Braino Inc.
227 Seminole Ave.
Wilkes-Barre, PA 18702

Writing support and editing: Eleanor K. Sommer
Cartoons: Robert C. Heim
Proofreading: Gillian Hillis
Design and production: Ludovica Weaver

Ellen Raineri
Wisdom in the Workplace
ISBN 0-9654035-0-5
Library of Congress Catalog Card Number: 96-96975

Produced, printed and bound in U.S.A.

# WISDOM IN THE WORKPLACE

## ON THE JOB TRAINING
## FOR THE SOUL

by
Ellen Krupack Raineri

*If your body gets injured at work, you get compensation. But if your soul gets wounded — hey you're on your own.*

Matthew Fox,
*Author of* The Reinvention of Work
*as quoted in the* Dallas Morning News

# ENDORSEMENTS

"*Wisdom in the Workplace* is wonderful! Ms. Raineri relates perfectly to challenges of the real world workplace, and she shares her leadership skills through her characters' dialogue. I related directly to the characters' emotions as I have experienced the same feelings on the job. I will definitely recommend this book to my colleagues at Christian Dior Perfumes, as it is surely a tool for the enlightenment of the workplace in the '90s and beyond."

Nancy VanDermark,
Account Executive, Christian Dior Perfumes

"*Wisdom in the Workplace* is a wonderfully and thoughtfully presented book that contains a genuine heartfelt message. The lessons of Wisdom are outlined in an engaging story-like format that is simple and accessible. *Wisdom in the Workplace* will be a valuable tool for every person who questions his or her role in the workplace."

Mark P. Downey, M.D., Chief of Anesthesiology
Vice President of the Medical Staff, Tyler Memorial Hospital

"Written in the spirit of Jonathan Livingston Seagull, this book addresses frustration in the workplace from a fresh, new angle — spiritual. Thought-provoking, insightful, and written allegorically, this book stands out among the dry, business texts on my bookshelf. Anyone searching for a much-needed, new approach should read *Wisdom in the Workplace*."

Dean T. Wenger, CPA

"Ms. Raineri has, perhaps unknowingly, been a teacher for me. I appreciate her teaching and writing as she presents a wealth of information in an understandable format. *Wisdom in the Workplace* reflects her impressive grasp of empowering concepts, obviously gained by her willingness to continually walk on Higher ground."

Cindy Shilanskis, Psychologist & Owner, A Woman's Place

"*Wisdom in the Workplace* presents an innovative, key approach to working through some of the wearisome challenges one experiences at work. A 'must read' for those in search of spiritual alternatives to make their 9-to-5 life more tolerable."

Carol Kelly, Administrative Assistant

"Usually we don't think of using unconditional love in the workplace as the workplace is seen as a formidable battlefield. *Wisdom in the Workplace* helps us keep situations in perspective and shows us that unconditional love can transform the situations."

Peterlyn Wojeska, TV, Radio, News Writer/Producer

"It is not our environment but our minds that determine our success. If we meet challenges openly and lovingly, they open us to an enlightened path. If we meet challenges closed and unlovingly, they become a darkened path. Ms. Raineri expresses herself lovingly and openly and is an enlightenment. Every business should have a copy and pass it on. *Wisdom in the Workplace* — a wonder for the soul."

Beverly Jean Johnston, Legal Administrator

"*Wisdom in the Workplace* is an informative, developmental journey for the evolution of one's soul; a wonderful journey benefiting every aspect of life in general."
Sandy Seyler, Holistic Practitioner

"*Wisdom in the Workplace* is fascinating and creative! Ms. Raineri offers a unique invitation to experience a vision of the workplace that echoes a seasoned rhythm of life. Ms. Raineri draws upon her experiences of ups and downs with honesty and insight. Through Ms. Raineri's guidance, we can find wisdom in wounds and attitudes that we have carried and also find spirituality in our everyday environment."
Linda S. Suponcic,
Office Manager, Unity Center for Positive Living

"*Wisdom in the Workplace* provides a comforting message to all who are confused and in pain from daily struggles in corporate life. Through her characters, Wisdom and Wonder, Ms. Raineri reminds us that challenges in the workplace are really paths of spiritual development, and by bringing this understanding to a conscious level we can reach a level of spiritual awareness that will pervade and strengthen all aspects of our lives. By gaining an understanding that our '9 to 5' lives are not simply meaningless manifestations of a material world but rather, 'schools' for the soul, we can begin to appreciate endless opportunities available to us for spiritual enlightenment and attainment of true peace of mind. Whether you are Wisdom or Wonder, you will be energized by Ms. Raineri's writing to share the wisdom and appreciate the wonder."
Peter DeYoe,
Manager, Information Technology Support Services

# Contents

*If I can stop one Heart from breaking*
*I shall not live in vain*
*If I can ease one Life the Aching*
*Or cool one Pain*

*Or help one fainting Robin*
*Into his Nest again*
*I shall not live in Vain.*

*Emily Dickinson*


*There's nothing in the world more powerful than an*
*idea whose time has come.*

*Red Motley*

## Author's Preface

During my business career, I have come to know the psychological pain and frustation associated with workplace challenges — both mine and that expressed by co-workers, bosses, and employees. It is the sort of pain that penetrates inner layers, anchors, and lasts for an unknown period of time. Being a jealous and commanding sort of pain, it demands an employee's full attention both in and out of work. Although physical and psychological manifestations often occur, employees more often maintain an underground conversation about their pain that is well hidden.

Where can relief be found? I wondered. Quitting is always an option, but this is especially difficult if you are in a specialized field, if you are not able to relocate, or if you really like other aspects of your job.

You can always go to your company's human resource department, unless, however, your company doesn't have one. You can access the Open Door Policy except that it may be closed. You can try to resolve the issues in a professional negotiation unless the office politics are too thick. Possibly an employee support group will help, but if you look around, you'll find support groups for alcoholics, for parents without partners, for people who want to lose weight but none for the abused employee.

What most of us do is cry on the shoulder of a sympathetic

employee co-worker, but each recollection of the workplace wounds seems to worsen the effect and length of pain.

So then, what on earth is an employee to do?

In my own search for pain relief, I did not find an earthly answer. My answer came from the realm of spirit — through a collection of wise ideas that business terms "principles," religion calls "rules," and spirituality reveals as "truths." I soon discovered that I could successfully apply these concepts in the workplace.

It is now my joy to be able to share these ideas with you. As you explore the ideas in *Wisdom in the Workplace*, you will come to realize you *can* cope with your job.

As you use these ideas, you will recognize a deeper level beyond the physical want of coping with a difficult boss or work scenario. You will find that survival in the workplace is really about creating a peaceful environment for your soul so *it*, too, can cope with *its* job. Because there is a physical and spiritual nature to our being, solutions must exist on both levels so we can not only survive but also move beyond basic job survival.

Some of my favorite wisdom books, *Jonathan Livingston Seagull*, *The Instant Millionaire*, *The One Minute Manager*, and *Raving Fans* have utilized a metaphorical tale to subtly convey a message. I, too, have chosen this form so that the lessons here may be meaningful as well as enjoyable. You will discern the secrets to success and survival that are just right for you as you follow the conversation between Wisdom and Wonder — the two primary characters that my dear editor has brought to life with her magic.

"There is no such thing as a problem without a gift for you in its hands. You seek problems because you need their gifts," Richard Bach tells us. Therefore, in this book are the "needed" gifts from the business problems that we face each day.

Wishing you much love and healing in the workplace,
*Ellen Krupack Raineri*

*No man is an island entire of itself.*

John Donne

# ACKNOWLEDGMENTS

Many thanks to the sacred group of people who have helped me "keep on keeping on," who have maintained for me the high watch, who have reminded me during the challenging times that "This too shall pass," and who helped me to practice what I wrote. I extend love and gratitude to Mary Krupack, Rev. Ann Marie Acacio, Carol Kelly, Peterlyn Wojeska, Sandy Seyler, Nancy VanDermark, and the Unity Circle of Prayer.

I extend love and gratitude to my immediate family, Mark, Mark, Brandon, Mary Krupack, and the late Jeanette Raineri who have accepted and supported me during the preparation, writing, marketing, and financing of my book. What a great extension of love, understanding, patience, and belief.

I extend love and gratitude to my fellow contributors of *Wisdom in the Workplace:* my editor, Ellie Sommer, for her brilliance, wit, creativity, and humor; my cartoonist, Bob Heim, for his humor, creativity, and artistic ability; Ruth Heim, for the humor and creativity that she has added in the thinking process; my proofreader, Gillian Hillis, for her eagle-eye; my designer, Ludovica Weaver, for her insight, creativity, and artistic ability; Gina Williams for the intelligence, business acumen, work ethics, and "good eye" that she has shared.

I extend love and gratitude to my endorsers: Alan Cohen, Gerald

Jamplosky, MD, Ken Blanchard, Mark Victor Hansen, Peter DeYoe, Dean Wenger, Carol Kelly, Sandy Seyler, Peterlyn Wojeska, Nancy VanDermark, Beverly Jean Johnston, Cindy Shilanskis, Linda Suponcic, Mark Downey, MD. Many thanks for your review, beliefs, and encouragement. I also extend love and gratitude to Shirley McNeill for her artistic design and talent that were shared in this endorsement phase.

I extend love and gratitude to a mixture of groups: The Osterhout Library and the reference librarians Sandra Schimmel, Diane Suffren, Elaine Stefanko, and Donna Fromel for processing my many requests for interlibrary loan books; La Tourelle and the general manager Leslie Leonard who has, although not planned, created a true writers' haven at this marvelous country inn in Ithaca, New York; the McNellis Co., New Brighton, PA and owner, Jerry McNellis, who have taught me compression planning, a tool that has assisted me with the marketing of my book; the Creative Problem Solving Institute (CPSI), Buffalo, New York, for the assistance in creative problem solving for planning many aspects of my book; and the Unity School of Christianity, the local Unity Center for Positive Living, and the Rev. Ann Marie Acacio who has taught me about success and survival on all levels.

# PROLOGUE

Wisdom

> "Wisdom cries out in the street;
> in the squares she raises her voice." *Proverbs 1:20*

> "Wisdom is the knowledge of things human and
> divine and of the causes by which those things are
> controlled." *Cicero*

> "Wisdom cometh by suffering." *Aeschylus*

Wonder

> "The man who cannot wonder, who does not
> habitually wonder (and worship) . . . is but a pair of
> spectacles, behind which there is no eye."
> *Carlyle*

Wisdom settled down in a comfortable chair in her office and beckoned Wonder to join her in a facing chair. She gazed at him for a time, and then turned her attention to the large window that framed her tidy, polished desk.

Her awareness brushed momentarily past the young man who waited nervously. She took in the blue sky and the white shredded clouds that glided past the window. She smiled inwardly at the sun as it shone abundantly on the green trees that surrounded the park beneath her office. The spring flowers were just beginning to bloom and she drank in their multicolored beauty.

Returning her full attention to her visitor, she surveyed his stiff figure. She did not need to see his wide eyes and damp brow to know his fear. She felt it. Wisdom let out a slow but hardly audible breath, hoping her release would relax her guest.

He had come to her hesitantly with an urgent request. He was drowning in a corporate sea, and he wanted her help with his career. They worked for the same company, a large multifaceted firm that specialized in mergers and acquisitions. It was an exciting diverse place to work with numerous opportunities in everything from tax and finance to transition management and human relations.

The company had even established a human relations department that worked directly with employees and managers in the transition stages of mergers and acquisitions. Wisdom felt proud that the company had the foresight to consider people in the transition package, but felt confused because this department still seemed, after many years, to be an "orphan." Little time and money was spent on developing this part of the business, although in her opinion, it was one of the major keys to a successful transition.

She surveyed Wonder, a relatively new recruit who she knew was bucking for a marketing position. He appeared to have the demeanor, although a bit untamed, to enter the fast-paced arena of high-tech financial deals. He was, Wisdom knew, at yet another crossroads in his young career. Wonder was about to leave the company — and he had been there less than a year. Things just didn't move fast enough for him. But this would be one of many jobs he had left, he had told her once as they chatted in the hall. And he really didn't want to repeat the pattern, he had confided. He thought he had left each previous position for good reasons: sometimes he couldn't fit in with his boss, other times it was fellow employees. But he was tired of starting over, and the problems seemed to be present in every job. So he had requested time with Wisdom, who had been at this company for years, in hope of some answers.

Wonder watched her hopefully. She seemed happy and successful and other employees had validated his observations. He would not leave until he knew how she did it. Wonder hoped she would tell him what to do.

"Well," Wisdom began, "how can I be of service, Wonder?"

"I . . . um . . . Well, I need to know how I can be successful? How can I move ahead in this company? Get my career into high gear?"

She smiled. *He is energetic*, she thought. *But he is going to have know when to drive and when to slow down.* She breathed in and out slowly one more time before answering.

"The answer is easy but not simple, and I can explain it in one word," she said as if telling him the riddle.

Words such as "patience," "enthusiasm," "imagination," and "perseverance" came to mind as he tried to guess Wisdom's "bullet" word. He looked at her, holding his breath, waiting for the magic word.

"Spirituality," she announced, looking him right in the eye.

He felt, in his face and in his stomach, the deepest disappointment and embarrassment when he heard that word — a word reserved for mystics, religious fanatics, Jesus Freaks, Holy Rollers — the weirdos. Yes, in his mind, weirdos covered them all.

Wonder thought perhaps he had misunderstood her, so he asked her to repeat the word.

"Spirituality," she said again, and Wonder's face and stomach repeated their queasy acrobatics. He felt it especially right under the middle of his rib cage, in the solar plexus.

Wonder shook his head and wished he hadn't asked for this

meeting and that he hadn't heard this answer. He thought he was unprepared for this path. *After all, they were in a business so how dare she talk about that here? How dare she embarrass him?* Questions flooded his mind.

*What could spirituality have to do with business? I need hard-core solutions,* he thought. But he knew he would have to be polite. He had initiated the meeting. He resigned to grit his teeth and get on with it.

Wisdom lovingly recognized the reaction in his face for she had seen it before in others who had come to learn the answer to business success and survival. Her eyes smiled and she validated Wonder's reaction.

"When you understand what I'm talking about, you will see how much this will help you in your job here — and even in your life in general. Wonder, I know some of these ideas will be uncomfortable at first, so I applaud you in advance for your open-mindedness and courage. I can teach you how to survive and be more successful in business. Are you interested?"

"Okay," he answered very quietly and somewhat hesitantly.

"Before we start our lessons, I invite you first to understand the three components of human beings: the body, the soul, and the spirit."

Wonder felt a little woozy but he tried to pay attention. He kept telling himself he did not have to return. He did not have to submit to the lessons, only to get through this one. He focused on her words and willed his mind to listen.

"The body is the exterior holder of the soul or an outer reflection of the *condition* of the soul. The condition of the soul may be expressed through the body in the form of happiness, love, depression, poverty, hurt, prosperity, loneliness, lack, humor, or fulfillment. The thoughts of the body are largely conscious thoughts because the body is in the material world interpreting through the intellect and judging by appearances and impressions. Judgment is important in our thought process but that judgment must be careful and correct. We have Jesus' words to teach us: 'Do not judge by appearances, but judge with right judgment.'" (John 7:24)

*There it is,* Wonder thought. *The Jesus stuff. I bet this is all going to be some lecture based on the Bible.*

Before his thoughts had even cemented in his mind, he heard Wonder saying — as if she had been reading his mind — "Of course, Jesus is not our only teacher. Life and history are filled with teachers. Wonder, you may find your teachers in the most unlikely places. But we will get to that later. Let me continue.

"Charles Fillmore, cofounder of the Unity School of Practical Christianity and another great teacher, came up with a definition of the second part of the human being:

> 'The soul touches both the inner realm of Spirit, from
> which it receives direct inspiration, and the external
> world, from which it receives impressions.'

The external world includes present conditions plus race consciousness: the collection of all beliefs, values, and limitations that have accumulated throughout time. The soul is a repository of both the conscious and subconscious thoughts. Does this body and soul talk make sense to you?"

"Well, not really. How can you know so much about the soul? It seems sort of impossible."

"Mmmm," was Wisdom's response. "Perhaps you'll begin to understand as we go along. Let me continue.

"The spirit is called by a variety of names depending on whom you reference: the Higher Self, the Best Self, the Christ, the Inner Self, our True Self, and the 'I am.' This spiritual part of us interacts with God or the Universe or the Divine, again the name depends upon personal preference. It connects us with our Source and then our lives can be perfect — if our souls and bodies are receptive. The spirit accesses superconscious thoughts through Divine ideas."

Wonder's mind reeled. *Here we are in la-la land. This is way too abstract to help me in my career.* He was beginning to feel sorry for himself.

"Wisdom, I do not mean to be rude, but this is just not what I had in mind. I..."

"Understandable. This is rather abstract. Please permit me to show you an example."

She sketched out a diagram on a piece of paper on her desk and turned it toward him.

"There."

This is what he saw:

Three Components of a Human Being:

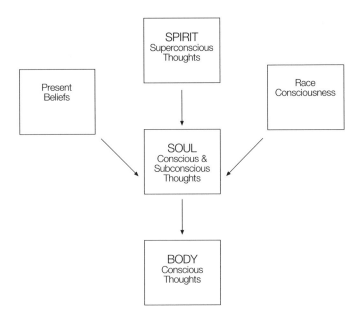

"You see how interconnected everything is? We cannot have a thought without there being a physical reaction. Our thoughts, desires, goals, and history are all tied up together. You can't sail into success, Wonder, without first examining how it all works!"

"Oh, I guess I sort of get it." Wonder said, beginning to accept the process. *Okay,* he thought, *maybe she can help me. But it better be fast. I'm on the career fast track and I've wasted enough time. Now I need to move on.*

"So when do I get to learn about business and spirituality and how this will help me get ahead?" he ventured, hoping to move things along.

"Soon. First, I'd like to teach you about the soul's evolution and its stages, about the school for the soul."

"School? For the soul? And this will help me in business?"

"It will. If you have patience."

Finally a word Wonder understood.

"Okay, so when do we start?"

"How about Friday. That'll give you a few days to think about what you wish to learn and to become adjusted to the idea of spirituality in business."

"See you Friday then," Wonder said as he rose from the chair. "And thanks."

Wisdom watched him exit her office. She laughed softly. She knew he was confused, but she was glad she had managed to interest him. She saw great potential in Wonder, if only he would relax and let in the information. *He has all the tools to be successful, he just doesn't know how to access them,* she thought.

*Every person, all the events of your life are there because you have drawn them there. What you choose to do with them is up to you.*

*Richard Bach,*
Illusions: The Adventures of a Reluctant Messiah

*. . . we choose our next world through what we learn in this one. Learn nothing, and the next world is the same as this one, all the same limitations and lead weights to overcome.*

*Richard Bach,* Jonathan Livingston Seagull

*Experience is a hard teacher because she gives the test first, the lesson afterward.*

*Vernon Law,* Pittsburgh Pirates Pitcher

# one

# THE EVOLUTION OF THE SOUL

Wonder arrived in Wisdom's office a little early on Friday. As he waited for her to finish up a phone call, he noticed how peaceful her office was. He chuckled at a cartoon on her desk. As she cradled the receiver, she smiled. Wonder smiled in return, still a little nervous.

"So, are you ready to begin your lessons?"

"I guess. I really want to be successful. I've tried everything. I guess at this point if you think spirituality is the answer, then I'll give it a try! So what about this school for the soul? Are there classrooms, grades, and stuff?"

He still felt kind of silly asking such questions, but he was curious about exactly what Wisdom was getting at.

"Of course," Wisdom said, explaining the types of subjects studied by souls: love, forgiveness, compassion, unconditional giving, detachment, endurance, nonresistance, assertiveness, humor, serenity, or surrender, for instance.

"It sounds like electives in college."

"Good comparison. You can certainly think of these as electives for the soul."

"And just who are the teachers for these electives?"

Wisdom was pleased. Wonder was being drawn into the conversation, and his initial hesitancy subsided as his natural curiosity emerged. Good, she thought and proceeded with her explanation.

"These subjects are taught by beings who may be difficult or easy teachers. When requested by the soul, these teachers present lessons. You've heard the expression, 'When the pupil is ready, the teacher appears.'"

"Oh sure," Wonder said, "but what does it mean exactly?"

"That when the soul is ready to learn certain lessons, the right teacher will come along whether or not the body thinks you are ready. Sometimes it's like a pop quiz; the body may neither want nor understand a particular lesson that a teacher presents. When a body resists a particular teacher, the body may attempt to drop out of that teacher's class. But sooner or later, a new teacher will appear. That new teacher may look different — it could be a teacher, a neighbor, a friend, a relative, or the clerk in the store down the road — but the same lesson will be presented until it is mastered by the soul."

Wonder took in this information for a minute. He regarded her with awe and respect, but he was still unsure about what he had gotten himself into. She was not that much older than he, perhaps ten years at the most, but she carried herself with authority and poise. He felt awkward and ridiculous and suddenly wished he had not asked for the meeting. He tried not to panic but quickly reviewed what she had just said and searched for a question to remove the pressing silence.

"Is it possible," he asked, "that our souls request teachers and our physical bodies are not aware that these people are teachers?"

"Yes. Usually we are not aware of these teachers unless we are focused on our spirituality and are considering each person we meet as a potential teacher."

"Are there grade levels, like a regular school?" He asked again, a little facetiously, and was startled by her serious answer.

"Yes. The soul chooses whether to remain at its current stage of evolution or to advance to a higher stage level. This advancement is accomplished by successfully passing various tests and examinations. Souls who choose to be fast learners and fast advancers receive lessons and tests at a very rapid rate. Thus, the human part of these souls may wonder why it receives so many challenges in life. This speed of advancement in the grade levels is discussed by Saint John of the Cross, who wrote:

"'Those who have the disposition and greater strength to suffer, He purges with greater intensity and more quickly. But those who are very weak are kept for a long time in this night, and these He purges very gently and with slight temptations.'"

Some of Wisdom's words were beginning to make sense. For years, Wonder had noticed business associates, the ones he admired, the ones who never hurt anyone, had frequent growing experiences. He now realized that their souls were "advanced." And, in retrospect, he now saw how those who "coasted" had few growing experiences.

## CLASSROOMS FOR THE SOUL

"Are we aware when our souls are graduating to a higher grade level?"

"Yes, once we recognize our soul's evolution, we know when we are advancing to a new level."

Wonder thought about this for a minute. It would be interesting to feel the movement of spiritual growth. He was surprised that he was even thinking along those lines. A few minutes ago, he had wanted to run from the office. Now his mind was beginning to fill with questions.

"Are there classrooms? Like homeroom, math, art, music?"

"Sort of. The school of life is divided into different types of classrooms so that the soul can effectively learn its lessons. Any subjects can be taught in any of the classrooms, but the tests and teachers may vary."

Wisdom outlined some of the classrooms for Wonder.

Finance Classroom

>Souls may experience tests such as unemployment, home repair bills, auto repair bills, college expenses, lost money, stolen money, or an inability to make ends meet.

Health Classroom

>Souls in this classroom may experience diseases, physical/mental pain, deformed body parts, or missing body parts.

Companion Classroom

>These souls may not be able to find the "right" person and may have marriages or relationships that don't last. These souls may be tested by "teacher" companions who cheat, who are unloving, who argue, or who are possessive.

Family Classroom

>Souls in this classroom are given tests by teachers such as in-laws, parents, children, brothers, sisters, uncles, aunts, cousins, or grandparents. Tests sometimes occur in the following areas: disobedience, narrow-mindedness, drug/alcohol addiction, unplanned pregnancies, jealousy, or hatred.

Career/Corporate Classroom

>Souls in this classroom have managers, employees, co-workers, recipients (patients, students, customers) who are teachers that are demanding, lazy, unappreciative, cheap, unfair, unqualified, slanderous, rigid, arrogant, and insensitive.

Wonder knew their discussion would focus on learning in the career classroom. "Is it possible for our souls to be in more than one classroom or to switch classrooms?"

"Our souls choose the classrooms in which they'd like to learn their lessons. And once you identify your classroom or classrooms, you start to identify fellow classmates. Some of the bodies in the class will merely be 'sitting in' on the class. However, other bodies are identified as souls who have also chosen that particular classroom for learning. Those bodies receive many tests and lessons."

"I know someone who keeps getting one career challenge after another. Is it likely then that his soul is in the career classroom?"

"It sure sounds like it," Wisdom said, smiling at her student. She saw his pain. Beneath his handsome face, she knew this young man was deeply troubled, but she also knew this act of reaching for help was the beginning of his recovery. He looked strong, and Wisdom sensed that his good looks had taken him places, but once there he floundered. His fear kept him from succeeding.

"Why all these tests? Tests are really stressful."

"To reinforce concepts and to measure retention, tests are given to the soul. Sometimes the tests are on material you are familiar with — books, classes, or earlier lessons. Other times, surprise quizzes are given to the soul. Often times, the body will remark that it had no idea that a particular challenge was going to occur. Exams, which are cumulative and more difficult, are presented before a lesson is concluded. Souls who are accelerated or who are in the advanced classes receive more difficult tests.

"St. John of the Cross supports this view with these words:

> "'. . . the nearer to God are the higher spirits and the lower, the more completely are they purged and enlightened with more general purification, and that the lowest of them will receive this illumination very much less powerfully and more remotely.'"

Wonder's mind raced. "Sometimes, I see classmates who experience extreme career challenges, worse than mine. It seems unfair. Why do they receive such extreme lessons?"

Wisdom did not answer right away. It was time her student began piecing together the puzzle. She decided to prod him with a question.

"Can you analyze what St. John of the Cross said? The nearer to God are the higher spirits, and the lower ones?"

"Let's see," Wonder ventured, "if I apply what you've just said, then I might now view the souls of these people as being very advanced souls and that is why they may be dealt such difficult tests."

She smiled. "You understand my words correctly."

"When I was in high school, I'd sometimes play hooky on the day of an exam. Can that also happen with souls?"

"Yes, souls also try to play hooky when they know they are being tested. They might cause the body to avoid a particular meeting or conversation they think might be difficult. However, just as in human school, makeup tests are given. Corporate souls may postpone but not skip tests. Eventually the test will be presented."

"So what's this school like?" Wonder asked, leaning back a little more comfortably in the chair. He was finally relaxing and enjoying his lesson.


EFFECTS EXPERIENCED DURING THE SOUL'S EVOLUTION

"This school may involve sacrifice or emotional, physical, or psychological pain. Again I turn to the mystic, St. John of the Cross who said, '. . . the soul is purged and stripped according to the spirit, and subdued and made ready for the union of love with God.' Here you can see how he discusses the dark nights in which the soul experiences sensual and spiritual purging."

Wisdom, herself, felt the need to pause here. She squeezed shut her eyelids for a moment and recalled the many times she felt her inside change from a rock under intense erosion to a yielding emptiness. She recalled the feeling of alignment that followed the yielding. It reminded her of being lined up for the "bunny hop" at a wedding! Her smile warmed with this silly image and she regained her composure to continue with another example for Wonder, who smiled back oblivious to her mini-excursion.

"St. John discusses more of the soul's painful experience in the analogy:

> "'. . . the soul feels itself to be perishing and melting away, in the presence and sight of its miseries, in a cruel spiritual death, even as if it had been swallowed by a beast and felt itself being devoured in the darkness of its belly, suffering such anguish as was endured by Jonas in the belly of that beast of the sea. For in this sepulcher of dark death it must needs abide until the spiritual resurrection which it hopes for.'"

Wonder winced. "It sounds excruciating — like the process of a painful death."

"As a matter of fact," Wisdom responded softly, "effects experienced from the evolution of the soul may be compared to 'mini-deaths.' This is due to diminishing of any number of human characteristics such as control, possessiveness, or addiction which is followed by a resurrection or a feeling of connection with our higher self."

Rubbing his chin in thought, Wonder reasoned silently, So in order for me to know the spiritual part of myself, certain physical qualities have to be removed or reduced. And out loud he said, "So every time we move from one level to another, we in essence 'die'?"

"Exactly. Another, mystic, Joel Goldsmith, speaks of this dying experience that is necessary during the evolutionary process of the soul:

"'The nature of God is I, that I which dwells in the midst of us, that I which we recognize to be individualized as our being. This I is not the body we see with our eye; it is not the egotistical I which believes that a human being has all power or that a human being is God but it is that gentle I which looks out from the center of our being. The human-centered I must 'die daily' that the divine I may be born again in us, and our divine relationships be revealed.'"

Wonder agreed. "So now I understand how our souls are affected during this evolution process. Overall, it sounds like an awful experience with a lot of inner pain. Does this death/birth process go on forever? Are there an infinite number of grades?"

"Not infinite, Wonder. It may seem that way at first. But there is an end in sight!"

## Results Obtained From the Soul's Evolution

> God looks into the mirror of the universe and sees
> Himself as man.
>
> *Charles Fillmore*

"Our souls are searching for their highest levels. The soul evolves so that it can graduate from all the grades. Graduation means no more teachers, classrooms, lessons, and tests. At graduation, the soul experiences 'enlightenment.' Shakti Gawain discusses this in her book, *Creative Visualization:*

> "'We may go through many different experiences and processes...but eventually we're restored to ourselves. That is, we come back into an experience of our true selves, the Godlike nature . . . that is within us all. Through this experience, we are eventually restored to

our full spiritual power, the emptiness inside us is filled up from within, and we become radiant beings, sharing the light and love that comes from within us with everyone around us. This is the process known as enlightenment.'"

"Okay. So we graduate and become enlightened. Is that it?" Wonder was beginning to think maybe this career spirituality stuff would be a snap and he could get on track without even messing up his wing tips.

"Not exactly," Wisdom said, amused at her student's sudden and sophistic burst of confidence. "There's more. We also gain the wise use of the various subjects we have mastered, which St. John of the Cross reminds us of: 'For if the soul be not tempted, exercised and proven with trials and temptations, it cannot quicken its sense of wisdom.'"

"Okay, so we graduate, become enlightened, gain wisdom and wise use of subjects. Does anything else result from the inner pain?"

"Sure. The final result is a oneness with God or a communion with the Divine."

"So we graduate, become enlightened, gain wisdom and wise use of subjects, and merge with God. Okay, I guess it's worth it."

"Glad you think so, Wonder. I guess it is clear that you and I are classmates in the career classroom. There are also many, many others who have made that choice for their learning environment.

"We've covered a lot of territory in one day, so I suggest that you finish your work here today — in your career classroom — and then go home and think about or meditate on all that you have realized during our conversation. And to help you, I've prepared a few notes to remind you of the lessons."

Wonder was amazed. Wisdom was so prepared, so together. He

watched her as she reached in her desk drawer and shuffled through a few papers. Her hair was neatly tied against the nape of her neck. Soft brown hair with bits of curls escaping from the clasp. Not unkempt, more like relaxed and joyous. Yes, that was it, Wonder observed. Somehow Wisdom had achieved a corporate attitude that was strong and assertive yet open and flexible. He felt new respect for his teacher and was sad the lesson was over.

He stirred from his reverie just in time to hear her asking, "Are you free on Monday evening to accompany me to an experimental theater production that is quite pertinent to the lessons we are discussing?"

"Well, uh sure," Wonder replied a little hesitant and nervous about a "social" outing with his new friend.

"Great, where should we meet?"

"Do you know where the Fifth Avenue Cafe is?"

"Sure. I'll meet you there at 7 p.m."

"See you then," Wonder said, glancing at the paper she had handed him.

Perhaps she had some answers, he thought, intrigued about what the next lesson might bring.

WISDOM'S NOTES TO WONDER

*And we all, with unveiled face, beholding the glory of the Lord, are being changed into his likeness from one degree of glory to another.*

*2 Cor. 3:18*

*The wood does not change the fire into itself, but the fire changes the wood into itself. So we are changed into God, that we shall know Him as he is.*

*Meister Eckhart*

*The seed of God is in us. Now the seed of a pear tree grows into a pear tree; and a hazel tree grows into a hazel tree; a seed of God grows into God.*

*Meister Eckhart*

*Into this dark night souls begin to enter when God draws them forth from the state of beginners — which is the state of those that meditate on the spiritual road — and begins to set them in the state of progressive — which is that of those who are already contemplative — so the end that, after passing through it, they may arrive at the state of the perfect, which is that of the Divine Union of the Soul with God.*

*St. John of the Cross*

## BIBLIOGRAPHY

Gawain, Shakti. *Creative Visualization.* New York: Bantam Books, 1978.

Goldsmith, Joel. *The Art of Meditation.* New York: Harper & Row, 1956.

John of the Cross, St. *Dark Night of the Soul.* New York: Doubleday, 1990.

*All the world's a stage.*
*And all the men and women merely players.*
*They have their exits and their entrances;*
*And one man in his time plays many parts.*
        *Shakespeare,* As You Like It. 2, 7, 139

*two*

# CAREER/CORPORATE STAGES

After a rather uneventful but hectic day at work on Monday, Wonder ducked out of the office shortly after 5 p.m. and raced to the dry cleaners on the way. He wanted to look his very best for his theater "date" with Wisdom.

When he arrived at the cafe, Wisdom was already there, sipping a cup of tea and reading.

"Well, good evening," Wisdom said. "You appear rested. I'm glad, because this trip to the theater will not be like others. I promise it will be exciting although possibly tiring."

"At the theater?"

"This is no ordinary theater, Wonder. It's an innovative repertory company that specializes in acting out challenges and scenes from various career and corporate situations. The company travels a lot to present to large corporations and business seminars, but when they don't have bookings, they perform locally."

"Wow, I've never heard of such a thing. What should I expect?" Wonder said.

"Well, I know that tonight's performance will be about the different ways people act out behaviors in their careers. It's not 'lite' theater, although you may find some of it sarcastically amusing. I did!"

"So, it's just like a play?"

"It's more than that Wonder. It's experiential."

"Experi-what?"

"Experiential. That means that the audience gets involved. The action often leaves the stage. It's a form of experimental theater," Wisdom explained.

"You mean... I might have to do something?" Wonder was even more nervous about that prospect.

Wisdom patted his hand. "Not to worry. You'll enjoy it. Let's get going so we can talk with people before the show starts."

As wherever she went, Wisdom met many friends and business associates in the lobby of the repertory company. Wonder occupied himself looking at the photos of previous shows that lined the wall of the lobby. It definitely looked to be an interesting group, he thought.

Eventually Wisdom located him and they headed toward their seats just as the curtain was rising. Wonder was filled with questions almost immediately.

## Fix 'Em Stage

"What classroom stage is this that is so busy?"

"This is the Fix 'em Stage. Business people have been challenged and they feel it's necessary to fix people who have challenged them. What do you notice about the actors?" Wisdom whispered.

"They look troubled, angry, and ugly. Some grit their teeth, spit, and curse. They also have large heads; I guess they are 'fixing' others by not sharing their business knowledge with others. Each actor is carrying around some sort of tool. What is that one?"

"A 'spiter' tool. She is using a spiter against business people who have presented her with challenges."

As they watched the various actions, Wonder recalled peers and business associates who used many of the tools being presented. Some of the tools he could not recognize.

"And what is that man's tool?"

Before Wisdom could answer, Wonder felt someone behind him poke his shoulder.

"Shut up, kid. Some of us want to hear the actors!"

Embarrassed, Wonder slumped in his seat a little just in time to hear the narrator begin to explain the scenes.

"And this person has selected an 'evener.' He has directed much of his energy into finding ways to get even with his teachers," the narrator said.

Wonder recalled a particularly loathsome character from his previous job: a loudmouthed fellow who more often than not said, "I don't get mad, I get even." And then he'd glare at you with a vicious eye. Wonder's attention returned to the stage. Another man stood in the spotlight, and the narrator continued.

"This woman's tool is a 'right server.' She carefully watches for seemingly negative experiences that her teachers have and doesn't miss the opportunity to interject 'It serves him right!'"

The audience's attention was next turned to another person with an odd looking tool that the narrator described as a "pay maker." "He has dedicated his life to finding ways to make his teachers pay dearly for every business challenge that has been presented to him."

Wonder considered this all while they waited for the next scene.

MAKEUP STAGE

> . . . prepare a face to meet the faces that you meet.
> T.S. Eliot, The Waste Land

"This is a colorful place. What's it called?"

"The Makeup Stage. What do you notice about the actors?"

"They're putting on makeup of different colors?"

"Right! Each actor selects makeup that depicts his or her reaction to the business homework and tests," Wisdom said.

A narrator took the stage and explained the significance of each color or shade:

"Masque is used to harden the areas around the eyes and lips to prevent smiling.

"White foundation is for the actors who choose to remain expressionless rather than letting others see their reaction to the surprise quizzes.

"Grey cream is for actors to use under their eyes if they have sleepless nights from worrying about how to complete their homework.

"Red cream is for actors to use around their eyes and noses if they cry over the difficulty of the tests.

"Dark cream is available for actors to use on their foreheads and between their brows if they are angry about the difficulty and frequency of homework and tests."

"Oh wow!" Wonder whispered. "How obvious, but still when they act it out... I mean point it out with makeup and actors and everything. It makes sense. Now I understand how we react to this unique school."

## PITY PARTY STAGE

Getting into the groove of the show, Wonder was ready when the next classroom appeared on the stage. The scenes were changed by a team of stagehands dressed in black, who seamlessly moved around as the new scene was set efficiently and artistically.

A lot of actors moved onto the stage and began roaming around. Wonder thought it looked like a party.

"We have been invited to a Pity Party classroom," the narrator confirmed. "Hear the wailing music of the violin. Notice the hearts that the actors wear on their sleeves."

Some of the actors began to move off the stage and wander among the widely spaced aisles.

"Why is that guy walking hunched-back, and why does he keep walking past me?" Wonder whispered to Wisdom.

"He wants you to pat him on the back. He thinks he has been taken for granted for years. He believes he has given to his company but received no recognition. Pat him, please."

Wonder did, but he felt strangely sad and resentful about it.

On the stage some actors were sitting at a table. There was a lot of noise, but Wonder couldn't figure out where it was coming from. Wisdom instructed him to watch the actors closely.

One was clicking her tongue making a noise of *tsk, tsk, tsk*. There were no party horns either. Instead, the actors blew their noses and cried in sympathy. When a guest of honor shared his business challenges, everyone pounded their fists and stomped their feet. Even the audience got into it. Pretty soon everyone was mumbling, "Oh, you poor thing," "How awful!," and "You have it so tough."

Wonder was grateful when the scene ended. Its cacophony and agony were more than he could stand.

## Giving With Pain Stage

> *There are those who give with pain and that pain is their baptism.*
>
> *Kahlil Gibran,* The Prophet

Wonder was more than ready for the intermission which thankfully came right after the Pity Party Stage. In the lobby, they sipped refreshing mineral water, and once in a while Wisdom introduced Wonder to a friend or acquaintance. Blinking house lights called them to their seats.

"Okay, what's next?"

"The Giving with Pain Stage," Wisdom said quietly, pointing to the program.

Wonder saw an employee talking and sharing information with his peers. As he talked, his head shrunk and he cried.

"This man was a longtime performer in the Fix 'em Stage. His head shrinks as knowledge is released. He has carried knowledge in his head like a woman carries a child in her womb. His releasing of knowledge is a birthing process as he learns about selfless giving," the narrator explained.

Although Wonder cringed at these scenes, he sensed their important messages. He wanted to jump ahead to understand it all right then. Wisdom must have read it in his face.

"Wonder, relax," she said calmly. "It will all be clear soon. I want you to see these things so that you will relate them to your real experiences and have an overview of the many ways in which we can open up to *or* ignore our spiritual lessons. Watch."

Next the actors strained to open and lift their arms as they tried to give. The audience heard voices yelling at the actors, but they were not coming from the stage.

From off stage, they heard: "She wouldn't help you so why are you willing to help her. . . ? You know your manager won't appreciate your hard work. . . . If you help her, she may get ahead of you. . . . Why waste your time helping your boss to look good. . . ? She's not worth it."

"Those are the ego voices of actors attempting to give through the pain. You hear the verbal battles of egos that do not wish to be tamed," Wisdom explained.

Wonder knew that battle well. Hardly a day passed that he did not see in himself and his peers the very actions described in the "play" going on the stage in front of him.

Next they saw a group of actors trying to give while bathing. However, that process did not appear to be a soothing, relaxing experience; they were screaming during their baths.

"Humility is the soap used for cleansing pride, and it stings when pride is washed away from giving," one of the narrators said.

Wonder wished humility could be experienced some other way.

## RUNAWAY STAGE

Next came the Runaway Stage. A narrator took the stage for a brief introduction.

"Here you will see actors try to leave a job or position before certain challenges are resolved. These actors have run away from challenges in the past and are still running. Do you see how tired and worn they look? They know where they want to go, but they can't get there. You probably wonder why. It's because they drag their baggage a few miles forward and then step backwards into the past."

"So is there something in the baggage that prevents them from going places?" said another actor who wandered onto the stage followed by a stream of actors trudging along with heavy loads.

"What's in their bags?" Wonder asked.

"Why don't you look in their bags?" Wisdom retorted as some of the actors dragged their sacks into the audience.

"It's okay to hold up the stuff for others to see," Wisdom prompted Wonder.

Wonder fished around in the bag and discovered a lot of old and worn clothing. He brought out one piece and held it up. On it was painted the word *hatred*.

The audience moaned. As the actor moved from person to person, more clothes were pulled from the bag. Many had a negative word inscribed on them such as *grudge, nonforgiveness, hurt, jealousy,* or *anger*. Some were neatly folded; some were faded and yellowed; and some were wrapped in plastic for preservation.

"I don't understand why they want to preserve such clothes," Wonder said.

"It's like preserving a wedding dress or a tuxedo. Runaways take out their saved memories to reminisce and try on experiences that fostered hatred, hurt, anger, jealousy, nonforgiveness, and grudges. Even though this baggage prevents them from getting where they are going, they continue to carry it because it is theirs and they are familiar with it," Wisdom explained.

"How sad to be stuck in the painful past and not to have the freedom of being able to experience the present good that is happening."

"Yes, Wonder, you have made an important observation. Remember it."


DOORMAT STAGE

Wonder was getting better at figuring out the stages. He began to make observations even before the scene was completely set up.

A narrator described the next scene.

"Look, all these actors are lying on their bellies — like doormats, but instead of WELCOME, the word VICTIM is imprinted on their backs. Other actors are walking over the ones lying down. Notice that the doormats are in groups. Are you curious why?"

Wonder couldn't really discern the groups. The stage looked like a mishmash, like a huge M.C. Escher painting, a complete mosaic of movement. He squinted and tilted his head. The narrator continued.

"See the backs of some 'doormats' are males and others are females. These are Gender Victims. Some doormats are different colors. These are Race Victims. And in the last group, you will notice that the backs of some of the doormats are wrinkled and some are smooth like those of adolescents. These doormats are Age Victims."

Wonder looked puzzled and turned to Wisdom.

"That's not fair. Doesn't gender, race, and age discrimination cause employees to be victims or corporate doormats?" Wonder's voice sounded agitated. Wisdom breathed and let silence pass before answering.

"Gender, race, and age discrimination are corporate dirt. If actors choose to absorb that dirt, they will then be doormats for other business actors to walk upon."

"Interesting to perceive that it is our choice."

This was a large thought for Wonder's brain to digest, and he missed some of the action while he was examining in his mind a person's complicity in his or her own discrimination. He thought about himself, and how he always imagined that he got a raw deal because of his youth or inexperience. *Maybe it wasn't really like that. Perhaps there is some merit to Wisdom's ideas,* he thought.


WITHDRAWAL STAGE

The narrator announced the next scene: "Here we are on the Withdrawal Stage. Notice how the actors are alone in their work environments. Business colleagues invite them to lunch, but these actors refuse; they eat alone at empty tables. Their colleagues attempt conversations, but these actors merely nod 'yes' or 'no.'"

Wonder knew a lot of people like the ones he was seeing. He always tried to talk to them, but they snubbed his attempts, or so he thought until now. He viewed those situations in a new light

He watched the next scene where another group of actors wore worried expressions as they looked in the air as if for an answer. Their eyes were angry and sometimes they shook their heads 'no' several times.

Juxtaposed to these scenes was a group of happy employees in a huddle; they tried speaking to a self-absorbed actor. The employees laughed and gestured for him to join them. He refused and closed his eyes.

"These actors have isolated themselves for they are in such pain that it can only be private," the narrator explained.

At that point in the play, the audience was invited backstage. They formed a line and went through the stage door to the backstage area where they walked around a dimly lit area.

Wonder was surprised. Backstage were actors who were too "weak" to perform even on the Withdrawal Stage. Some had tape over their lips so their colleagues would not even consider asking about their career challenges. Some actors wore patches over their eyes and plugs in their ears so that they could not see or hear their colleagues' gaiety.

"These actors are very weak," Wisdom whispered as they walked by.

"I hadn't realized that pain can cause such isolation," Wonder mumbled under his breath as they walked back to their seats.


RESCUE STAGE

"There's one more scene," Wisdom told Wonder as they returned to their seats.

"This is the Rescue Stage," the narrator boomed across the stage. "The power of these employees' challenges has reached the emergency level, and they have pressed the RED ALERT button to call for help. What do you see?"

Wonder was alarmed when he looked around. Adrenaline rushed through his veins. On one side there was someone on fire yelling for help. On another side was an actor drowning. In the back was a woman in a simulated earthquake. She was screaming.

The narrator waved his hand and the noise level dropped but continued as he spoke.

"This may look awful, but each part has a purpose. The man on fire is being challenged by his manager and feels that the 'heat' is on.

He doesn't know how to escape the situation so he gets badly burned. One of his scars will be called 'generalizations' for he will avoid similar situations with managers, saying 'I've gotten burned before and I'm afraid I'll get burned again.'

"And the fellow drowning once had control over his challenges with clients but now those challenges and that control are filling up his world. He feels that things are over his head as he sinks to their power.

"The woman in the earthquake once felt that her career was on solid ground. Then the challenges happened. Now, she walks with shaky steps as her world crumbles to her feet and she no longer understands the new rules of corporate politics."

Wonder was breathless. As quickly as the narrator would explain a disaster, he would spot another one. He saw an actress in a room without electricity; she was panicking and crying for help.

"That woman," the narrator said solemnly, "saw clearly what was happening for light illuminated her work place; now she feels her coworkers have left her in the dark. She does not attempt to move through her challenges. Instead, she stumbles and falls to the power of the obstacles."

A loud crash echoed through the theater from behind the audience. Everyone turned around just in time to see a guy falling from a ladder. Several people including Wonder stood and shouted, "Look! Be careful. Watch out."

They realized in an instant that it was part of the play. Wonder felt a little embarrassed and slouched back down in his seat. Wisdom smiled.

The narrator explained: "For years, this man has gained strength to lift his legs to reach higher rungs on the corporate ladder of success. Then the challenges came and pushed him. As he falls, he recalls the effort and games associated with each business achievement and realizes that it is indeed a long way down. He does not know if he will be able to climb again."

Just when Wonder decided he couldn't take any more excitement, he heard the screeching of brakes, the crashing of metal, and breaking of glass. Savvy to the tricks, he turned his attention back to the stage where he saw a woman in an auto accident.

"Sometimes an actress sees her career challenges approaching and sometimes the career challenges take her by surprise," the narrator offered. "That's the case here. The result has a varying impact. In some cases, the power of the challenges can 'total' a life. In other cases, it leaves dents, and in others, it merely scratches the surface."

Wonder closed his eyes. It was too much. "So... is there a 911 crew to come to their rescue?" he whispered to Wisdom. He sincerely hoped so.

"Very thoughtful question, Wonder. Actually, souls are responsible for rescuing themselves, but there are some souls who teach us rescue methods but do not actually do the rescuing."

The narrator affirmed Wisdom's words, and called all the actors and actresses back on stage where they were greeted with a standing ovation.

Wonder knew that Wisdom had taken him to this play as a lesson and that there must be a way out — at least for those who choose to recognize the cycle of pain and frustration in the workplace and make an effort to overcome it.

As they exited the theater and waited for a cab, Wonder asked how an actor can be promoted out of one of the classrooms he had just witnessed.

"The actors' souls move when they learn the lessons. Study aids are available to help the souls advance. We'll talk about that next week. That's when we'll get into more practical discussions, learn to 'walk the talk,' as they say. In the meantime, get some rest. Today's lesson was very intense. Rest for a few days. Let's get together again next Monday at the office."

Wonder smiled. "Thank you. I look forward to practical lessons. I need to know how to do these things. See you next Monday."

*Spirituality, unconditional love, and the ability to see that pain and problems are opportunities for growth and redirection — these things allow us to make the best of the time we have.*

*Bernie Siegel, M.D.*

*Remember the Greek saying that character strength comes from a long process of dealing with adversity. Character is the result of countless hours of dealing with difficulties in a constructive way. Unfortunately, it isn't a quick process.*

*Brian Tracy*

*The world breaks everyone and afterward many are strong at the broken places.*

*Ernest Hemingway*

*Difficulties and responsibilities strengthen and enrich the mind.*

*William Lyons Phelps*

*Adversity causes some men to break; others to break records.*

*William Arthur Ward*

*three*

# DIAMONDS, PEARLS, AND PEONIES

Refreshed from the weekend, Wonder bounded into the office Monday morning, and after spending some time with his work, he headed for Wisdom's office.

"Oh, good morning Wonder," said the familiar voice of Wisdom's administrative assistant. "Wisdom asked me to let you know she'd like to meet you in the break room. Looks like you got some sun this weekend."

"Yeah, spring's finally here. I got in my first round of golf Sunday. Thanks, see you later."

Wonder ambled toward the break room on the seventh floor, which he knew to be one of the best in the building. Not only did it overlook the park, but the architects had designed a patio/atrium that provided a restful place for employees to have coffee or lunch.

Just as he suspected, Wisdom was sitting at one of the outside tables reading *The Wall Street Journal*. He poured himself a cup of decaf and joined her.

"Hi," he said as he drank in the fresh breeze and appreciated the blossoms on the potted dogwood behind Wisdom's chair.

"Wonderful morning. Nice to be alive, don't you agree?"

Wonder regarded her eternally optimistic nature, hoping one day he might acquire the same. He joined her at the table as she put away the paper.

Opportunities

> *The marvelous richness of human experience would lose something of rewarding joy if there were no limitations to overcome. The hilltop hour would not be half so wonderful if there were no dark valleys to traverse.*
>
> *Helen Keller*

"Wonder, I'd like you to think back and tell me about the challenges that you have experienced or have seen other actors in the corporate classroom."

Wonder thought for a moment, and then scribbled down some ideas on a notepad he had brought along. Friday's information had been so intense, he decided he should take notes. After a while, he pushed the pad toward Wisdom.

She looked pleased as she surveyed his list:

Being

+ bypassed for a promotion that was deserved
+ criticized publicly
+ intentionally excluded from meetings
+ overworked
+ blamed for someone else's ineptness

Having

+ someone else steal the recognition for work completed
+ your pay decreased so your boss's can be increased
+ to complete meaningless paperwork
+ an unfair performance review

Not being

+ appreciated
+ empowered

- taken seriously
- appropriately compensated

Working

- for a boss who steals accounts or employees
- for a boss who threatens you if you use the open door policy
- for a boss whose prejudice is uncontrolled
- for a threatened manager
- for someone who is authoritative
- with or for a manager who is two-faced
- with or for someone who fakes her knowledge
- with someone who 'kisses up' to management
- for a company that is closed to new ideas
- for a company whose ethics are different from your own

"How do you feel about the challenges you put down here?"

"They're horrible and painful experiences to endure! Sometimes I think I'm the only one who has had such experiences."

"Wonder, I can tell you from personal experience that is not true."

Wonder regarded his teacher. *How could she have any such experiences? She appears so serene and calm.*

"Really? Like what?" Wonder asked fully expecting to hear about some trivial office hassle.

"Well," Wisdom began, "once I was trying  change a situation I found myself in. You see, my boss, at the time, felt insecure about his position and felt very uncomfortable with my thorough knowledge of certain aspects of the job. I wished that it weren't the case, and I made a point of *not* discussing books I read. I didn't even hang my degrees on the wall in an effort to ease the tension. It was no use."

"You knew more than he did?"

"Not about everything, Wonder. I even made a point of jotting down questions about areas I knew he was knowledgeable in so I could ask him questions. I figured I'd learn something and my boss would feel more secure in his position."

"Sounds as if you really tried!"

"I did. I wanted to get him to understand me, to let him know how much I wanted to do a good job and to be recognized."

"And so what happened?"

"I was finally able to schedule a meeting, and I decided to add some spirituality in the form of generosity. After all, *giving* unlocks the door to unconditional love. I decided to create a special gift for the manager and his family — some strawberry cheese croissants and fresh strawberries. Days before, I ordered the croissants just to make sure the bakery had not sold out. The night before our meeting, I picked up the croissants but the strawberries were overripe so I went to another grocery store for them. I searched several stores to find just the right gift bag and just the right red ribbon. On the day of meeting, I waited in front of our building for the manager to pick me up. I waited forty-five minutes. I waited until a co-worker came out to tell me that he had called to say he couldn't make our meeting because he had been detained out of town. There was no mention of rescheduling. I gave the croissants and strawberries to the doorman."

"What a lesson! How did this help you to grow?"

"I learned not to go where I am not wanted and not to try to be with people who do not want me. Unfortunately, it took me a while to learn that lesson. I tried to schedule other meetings or leave phone messages. Similar episodes resulted."

"I don't understand, Wisdom. If I am embarrassed or criticized in public or bypassed for a promotion, how can I see those situations in a nonpainful way?"

"Perhaps we can learn the answer in words from Epictetus: 'Men are disturbed, not by the things that happen, but by their opinion of the things that happen.'"

Wonder looked puzzled. He sort of understood but not completely.

"You see, Wonder, it all depends upon how you *perceive* the challenging work situation. You may choose to see opportunities for greatness in any corporate challenge. Of course, the key word is *choose* for it's much easier to choose to feel embarrassment, anger, bitterness, or jealousy because we do not readily see or believe that good is part of every situation."

"Your words sound familiar. Reminds me of an anonymous saying: 'Every problem is an opportunity in work clothes.'"

"Exactly!"

Wonder beamed with pride. He *was* getting it! His interest focused.

"Okay. Let's say that I buy into the idea that there are opportunities in corporate challenges. But opportunities for what? I'm not a masochist."

"Opportunities for three things. First, opportunities for making achievements in your life. Challenges are an impetus to greatness. Think of a rocket's need for the launching pad to propel it into space or the diver who needs a springboard to propel himself into the air and into the water. Use your challenges as your launching pad. William Clement Stone, a writer, speaker, and president of Combined Insurance tells us, 'Stop and think about it for a moment. Do you know of a single instant where any real achievement was made in your life that was not due to a problem facing you?' And Eric Butterworth, author of *Spiritual Economics* tells us, 'Many have suspected that their achievements came not in spite of their challenges, but as a result of them.' Learn to examine your challenges and to really use that pain. Challenges can be painful; do not waste that pain. Use it as the foundation of your greatness."

"Who could possibly make achievements because of challenges? I thought only lucky people have that good fortune."

Wisdom tempered the tinge of annoyance that tried to surface in her. How often had she heard that excuse from people who were not successful?

"Wonder, let me assure you there are no *lucky* people. *You* are responsible for creating the positive or negative results in your life by the manner in which you speak, think, and act. You are, at each moment, experiencing a boomerang effect."

"What's that?" Wonder asked.

"Any positive or negative words, thoughts, or actions always come back to you! You know, what goes around, comes around?"

"Oh, yeah. I get it."

"So let's get back to the challenges that help us in our careers. There are many great achievers who have 'made it' because they successfully deal with their challenges. Consider Thomas Edison. He refused an ear correction and he used his deafness as a tool for better concentration. Louis Braille, blind since he was three years old, developed the Braille system so the blind may read with their fingers. Many motivational speakers became great due to their search to overcome challenges. And remember the great authors who wrote works while in jail: John Bunyan, *Pilgrim's Progress*; Miguel de Cervantes, *Don Quixote*; Daniel Defoe, *Hymns to the Pillory*; O. Henry, collection of short stories; and Oscar Wilde, *Ballad of Reading Gaol*."

"Okay. I see your point. I guess our challenges can be the foundation for our greatness. So what is the second opportunity resulting from our challenges?"

"The development of virtues. Our virtues strengthen themselves as we practice using them. So, think for a moment, Wonder, what sort of virtues do you think can be developed from experiencing challenges in a positive manner?"

"I suppose our survival skills and our level for tolerating pain can be improved."

"Yes, but there are many more virtues. What else?"

Wonder turned again to the pad, but Wisdom stopped him.

"Notes are good, Wonder, but this isn't a test. Sit back. Relax. Close your eyes, and just imagine some virtues and say them aloud. Feel them in your mind. Hear them as you speak. Review them again and again."

He felt a little silly, but so far Wisdom had not let him embarrass himself. He did glance around just once to see if anyone else was on the patio.

"Okay. Here goes: Patience . . . umm . . . humor . . . a positive mental attitude . . . understanding . . ."

Suddenly he had the hang of it, and the rest tumbled out easily: "Empathy, open-mindedness, wisdom, tact, perseverance, self-dependency/appreciation, creativity, humility, balance."

"Very good, Wonder! So you see how great challenges can be?"

"Well, I still don't like challenges. Why can't we just be born with all these virtues or just buy them like a new car or clothes?"

Wisdom looked at her student. *Impulsive*, she thought. She saw his desire to be where he wasn't, to skip the path and get right to the goal. Not an unusual human trait, she mused.

"It would seem easier, but I think the result would not be the same. The way to acquire a high level of a particular virtue is by successfully enduring or moving through a challenge to *earn* that virtue. For example, think how any person develops the virtue we call patience — by waiting in traffic lines. How does the salesman develop patience? By successfully dealing with rejections from clients. How can an employee who was bypassed for a promotion develop perseverance? By discovering other avenues or by strengthening other skills so that he or she achieves greatness at the same or a different organization. Think how the laid-off employee develops creativity to devise an outstanding business in response to the question, 'How will I be able to support my family?' Last, think how all of the challenged employees develop a strong sense of humor as the only way to survive the pain and frustration of the corporate stage," Wisdom concluded.

"Sounds like the successful business people who are also admired because of their wisdom, creativity, perseverance, and other virtues have had a tough road."

"You're exactly right! Success is not an easy process. And it often is built upon virtues that are acquired through pain. Please remember that statement whenever you see successful people and feel a tinge of envy."

Wonder sighed.

"Yes?" Wisdom inquired.

"Well, it's just that you seem so peaceful and adjusted in your job. I can't see that you had to go through any of this stuff."

"Oh, Wonder, you have no idea how difficult it has been!"

"So, what have been some of your challenges?"

"Too numerous to name. But here's an example. My boss once shared with me that he competed with me for clients' projects rather than supporting me. He reassigned clients to himself to increase his bonus payments, even though in fact, I still did the transition work with those clients, sometimes working through weekends and evenings to ensure smooth operations when two companies merged," Wisdom confided.

"So here you have a manager who is not managing you but who is competing with you, who doesn't push you up the career ladder but who instead tries to stop you or knock you down," Wonder sounded exasperated as he summarized Wisdom's position. "I'm curious what lesson you learned from this test?"

"I learned how to appreciate *myself* and have confidence in myself even though my boss did not believe in me. I believed in myself and in my success. I also learned about inner strength so that I could move through or around people and obstacles. And finally, I learned about prosperity. Even though my boss closed off my avenues for prosperity, I was able to open others that were even more lucrative."

"How did you increase your inner strength?"

"Several ways. I increased my strength and power through meditation. Typically I spend one and a half hours a day practicing success strategies. It is my belief that if meditation is done regularly, we stay more emotionally balanced and other people and situations are easier to handle. Through meditation, we can increase our inner stance so we do not wobble in the face of adversity."

"Tell me about a typical meditation session." Wonder requested.

"First, I get in an alpha state, either naturally or through counting from one hundred backwards to one. I meditate in silence or with relaxing music. In the alpha state, I repeat positive statements that help me. I focus particularly on strength. As mentioned earlier, various colors carry with them energy. The color red carries with it power and strength. I might visualize red energy combining with my heart's energy filling my inner body and surrounding my outer body. I might use a red candle to further increase the power and strength."

"How were your interactions after your daily meditations?"

"Better, they didn't leave me as exhausted. I dealt powerfully with the obstacles he placed in my career path."

Wonder took in all this new information carefully. Wisdom allowed him time to analyze this real-life information. Shortly, Wonder stirred in his chair and asked Wisdom to continue. "So what is the third opportunity resulting from our challenges?"

"The third and most important opportunity is an opportunity for us to advance spiritually. 'And all of us, with unveiled faces, seeing the glory of the Lord as though reflected in a mirror, are being transformed into the same image from one degree of glory to another' (2 Cor. 3:18). You see, Wonder, each time we overcome challenges in a positive manner, we advance ourselves to higher spiritual levels. The ultimate level, of course, is the Sacred Self level — where we continuously experience a oneness with our God nature," Wisdom concluded.

"I hear you speak of the opportunities resulting from challenges —achievements, virtues, and spiritual advancement. This seems so painful. I think it would be easier to be an inanimate object or a plant."

"Sorry, Wonder. You have a misperception. Many of nature's greatest elements —the ones that are considered beautiful and perfect are that way as a result of *challenges*. I can think of three right off the top of my head: the diamond, the pearl, and the peony."

"Well, you're going to have to explain, because now you've really lost me," Wonder said good-naturedly.

GEMSTONES AND FLOWERS

> *Sweet are the uses of adversity*
> *which like the toad ugly and*
> *venomous wears yet a precious jewel*
> *in its head and this our life*
> *exempt from public taunt*
> *finds tongues in trees*
> *books in the running brooks*
> *sermons in stones and good in everything.*
> *William Shakespeare*

"Consider for a moment a diamond. Just like coal, graphite, and charcoal, it is composed of carbon and is formed through the extreme heat and pressure of the earth upon fallen trees. It takes millions of years for the diamond, carbon in the form of crystals, to form. But even after that ordeal, diamonds are still not complete. They are cut in many surfaces or facets. The actual beauty of a diamond is realized by the way in which it reflects the light; well-cut diamonds reflect the colors of the rainbow. In terms of value, diamonds with flaws are worth less than diamonds without flaws. And finally, diamonds are considered to be very hard substances — five times harder than any man-made substance."

"How does that relate to spiritual advancement?" Wonder asked.

"Our lessons often put us under extreme heat or pressure. We may even identify with the expression, 'The heat is on.' And while it may not be millions of years, it can sure seem like a lifetime or lifetimes that we are under this heat."

"That's for sure!"

"And after this pressure treatment, like the diamond, we may find ourselves cut and shaped as various personality traits are sliced from us. These may include ego, resistance, personal will, or ignorance. Perhaps we are aware of the replacements which are facets of light called humility, nonresistance, divine surrender, or wisdom. When some of our ego is sliced away, we can reflect the light which is the light of the Divine for we are created in the image and likeness of His being. Just like the diamond, we are worth more as spiritual beings when we have fewer flaws."

Wonder noticed a large marquise diamond on Wisdom's slender hand. He knew from that point forward diamonds would have a special meaning for him. Wisdom continued her explanation.

"The last point in the analogy focuses on the hard quality of diamonds. There is a certain degree of hardness or strength that we develop in our spiritual evolution. That hardness or strength comes from developing and pairing our twelve powers."

"Twelve powers?" Wonder asked.

"Oh, yes. We haven't talked about those yet, have we?"

Wonder shook his head.

"Well, rest assured that you haven't missed anything from your graduate school's curriculum. The twelve powers are from, shall I say, the spiritual curriculum. Since you have a pen in hand, you might write down *The Twelve Powers of Man* by Charles Fillmore, in case you'd like more information than what I have time to share with you today."

Breathing in a few long breaths, Wisdom arranged her thoughts for a brief explanation.

"Wonder, in our bodies, we have twelve inner powers that are located at twelve physical nerve centers such as the center of the brain, the pit of the stomach, the back of the heart, and others. These twelve powers include faith, strength, judgment, love, power, imagination, understanding, will, order, zeal, elimination, and life. In addition to each power being represented at a physical nerve center, it is also represented by a particular apostle. There are techniques that can be utilized to further activate a particular power if it seems to be blocked in the nerve center."

This was a lot for Wonder to swallow, but so far Wisdom had guided him to useful paths.

"So you said these powers are paired. What does that do?"

"Our powers work best when they are utilized in pairs since this creates a natural strength and balance. For example, balancing love and wisdom makes us strong or hard so that we can face any corporate challenge successfully. Balancing will and understanding helps us to make better business decisions, and so on."

"Remarkable analogy! And I thought that diamonds were just automatically stunning! So what other objects can we explore so I can understand about this work involved in success?"

"What do you think about pearls, Wonder?"

"They're beautiful, very durable gems. But I bet you have a story about them."

"Well, you're right! An oyster is an easygoing fellow who secretes a substance called *nacre*. Whenever sand gets under its shell, an irritation results. As I'm sure you learned in school, when the oyster cannot get rid of the irritation, it releases nacre to cover the sand, which then changes the sand or irritation into a pearl. And when someone is lucky enough to discover an oyster shell with a pearl inside and lifts it out into the sunlight, the pearl glistens with the colors of the rainbow. Occasionally, there are blemishes on the pearl and skillful artisans called peelers scrape away the blemishes so that the pearl becomes even more valuable. Unlike the diamond, the pearl is soft and easily scratched."

"I'm starting to get it, but I need you to make the connection for me, again."

"No problem. Haven't you sometimes felt an irritation — like something under your shell or skin? You try to get rid of it, to no avail. The irritation might be a manager, an employee, a client, or a corporate situation. When we realize that the irritation is not going to go away, we may try to see the good in the situation. Many famous writers have done this as I shared with you earlier."

"So how does a pearl's development relate to spiritual advancement?"

"Like the oyster, we can choose to change our irritation to a pearl. Of course the key word is *choose* for as I have mentioned; it's much easier to be sad, angry, or devastated from our business irritations. We can create all sorts of pearls: patience, humor, a positive mental attitude, empathy, open-mindedness, perseverance, tact, wisdom, creativity, humility, or intuition can be the result of irritations. With our spiritual advancement, we, too, reflect light, the light of the Divine within us, and demonstrate a rainbow brilliance as shown in our surrounding auras. Perhaps during our evolution, we, too, may have blemishes like the pearl. And people may enter our lives to peel away our blemishes.

"But what about the softness of the pearl? Could that be an asset?" Wonder probed.

"Ideally, we'd like to acquire the hardness and strength of the diamond. However, during our evolution, we do not automatically attain a balance between our twelve powers. There are times in which our powers are overbalanced or under-balanced and we are soft or easily scratched. For example, our Love faculty may be overbalanced and not paired with Wisdom so we become a corporate 'yes person' and may allow ourselves to be walked over like the actors in the Doormat Stage. Other people may regard us as being so nice and soft but we are being scratched. Similarly, if our Will faculty is overbalanced and not paired with Understanding, we make ego centered decisions that we may later regret."

Wonder stood for a moment to stretch. Wisdom left the table to refill her tea, pinching off a piece of Danish to enjoy with it. Their time was nearly up, and she had a lot more ground to cover.

Wonder was waiting for her when she returned. "So now you have to tell me about the flower, the peony," he said.

"A wonderful flower. It is dormant in the ground during the winter, but its perennial flower grows up from the same roots every year. Even though it grows up from the ground, it will not blossom if it is not helped by irritating ants. The peony has all its petals clustered in a ball, and the ants, drawn to the aromatic inner part of the peony, use their feet to pry back the petals. The ants help the peony with its unfoldment so that outer physical beauty and inner aromatic beauty is manifested."

"Wow! Wisdom, now that I've heard you make two analogies, may I attempt to formulate this third one?

"Of course," uttered Wisdom, not hiding the slight pride she felt in her student.

"Okay. Here goes. I suppose that we might be regarded as somewhat perennial beings. However, instead of every year, it is every lifetime that we come out of dormancy and grow up again from the same roots of our Divine Self. Does that sound right?"

"Yes! And what do you suppose the ants represent?"

"The irritating people and challenges that are drawn to our inner nature — the God nature, as you call it. I suppose they are helping us to unfold our petals of nonresistance, patience, wisdom, love, and so on, so that our inner beauty can be seen."

"Excellent analogy!"

## P.S. BLUE JEANS, TOO

"Wonder, before we leave these analogies, I have one more to share: blue jeans!"

"Blue jeans? This I gotta hear."

"Jeans can acquire excellent, comfortable, and worn nature in two ways. First they can be worn and washed for many years. But this same nature can come about after an acid bath, which is much quicker. In either case, the jeans become relaxed, comfortable, and softened. Wonder, would you like to try to discuss the analogy?"

"I haven't a clue on this one so I'll pass."

"In the career classroom, some actors' challenges last a long time, perhaps several years. For those actors, their spiritual development is like jeans that have been softened by years of usage. Other actors are challenged intensively over a short time, similar to that of the acid washed jeans. In either development process, the result is a visibly worn inner look. When that happens, these people are comfortable to be with for they are not stiff or inflexible. This 'wearing' process is absolutely essential for spiritual development for when our souls are worn or acid washed, then we are able to yield to the direction or guidance of God."

"That's a neat analogy. But what about the patches on jeans?"

"Super question! Patches can be part of this analogy, too. Patches are applied to areas that are worn thin from usage, typically knee areas. The patch then makes a weak area one of the strongest areas of the jeans. In our spiritual growth, perhaps corporate challenges may be so intense that we go beyond the depth of being worn. We may 'come apart' or function by 'bare threads.' Then, perhaps a blessed someone comes into your life and offers you a 'patch' of love, confidence, power, or support. And perhaps that patch becomes the strongest part of your development."

WALKING THE TALK

"Wisdom, I know it is late, and we both have to get back to work, but you mentioned Friday that you would be giving me some practical advice about making these connections and about my struggles in this corporate classroom."

"What we need are 'shields' to help to deal with this stuff. And here they are." Wisdom removed from her canvas briefcase a few neatly typed pages.

"You can read these tonight, and then at our next meeting if you have any questions, we can go over them. But I think you'll find them quite self-explanatory. Oops. Gotta go. I have a meeting at eleven."

She moved quickly and elegantly to the door and vanished down the hallway.

Wonder decided to finish his coffee and look over the list before returning to his desk.

Choose to find the bright side of any challenge. I suggest that as a key to seeing the sunshine, you make an effort to list the positive or good sides of challenges.

*Keep your face to the sunshine and you cannot see the shadow.*

*Helen Keller*

Be willing to accept the challenge but realize that it will end sometime and that during its existence, it need not have any power over you.

*Finally, whatever is true, whatever is honorable, whatever is just, whatever is pure, whatever is pleasing, whatever is commendable, if there is excellence and if there is anything worthy of praise, think about such things."*

*Philippians 4:8*

*I accept the reality of this situation but not its permanence.*

*Eric Butterworth*

This too shall pass.

*You may not be able to keep the birds from flying over your head, but you can keep them from building nests in your hair.*

*Anonymous*

*The economic depression has no power over my sales. I create outstanding marketing opportunities. I claim my wealth.*

*Ellen Raineri*

Realize that you are not a victim to other people or situations. You have the power to be a corporate survivor.

*Endurance — we are never given more than we can handle. In fact, we are given exactly what we need at any given time.*

*Anonymous*

You might consider making a mini-poster of these words or print them on an index card.

Read them throughout the day. Affirm to your-self, "I successfully handle this and any challenges that pass through my life. I claim this power through my Inner Essence."

Read books that are based upon positive thinking and spirituality. Read magazines such as *Unity Magazine, Success, Personal Selling Power, Daily Word,* and *Science of Mind* that instill confidence and encouragement. In these types of books and magazines, you will encounter preserved wisdom, a key to your survival in the corporate classroom. Use that wisdom to shield you.

Make yourself a success tape filled with affirmations. You may even wish to play relaxing music in the background while you state your affirmations.

Know that it is darkest before the dawn. The most challenging period of your spiritual growth precedes the calming advancement level. People often give up right before their success is to be realized. Try the very simple words of Eric Butterworth: "Keep on keeping on."

Realize that you may be receiving a Divine nudge to make a change. Consider the mother bird who wants her baby bird to fly. The babies have no incentive to fly away, for they are com-fortable in the nest and they are being fed. The mother bird sometimes puts small, sharp objects such as glass into the nest. Soon, the babies choose to make a change, even though they were once comfortable in the nest. In our own spiritual lives, we are sometimes presented with what I call "divine uncomfortables" that nudge us into making a change. Use change as a shield to bring you to your greater good.

Realize that peace of mind is one of the most valuable qualities that you can have. You attain peace of mind by how you interpret or energize outer experiences. For example, if your co-worker does not reciprocate your morning greeting, you may choose to feel anger or you may choose to protect the peace within your mind. From *A Course in Miracles*, try the phrase, "I can choose peace instead of this."

Also consider the occurrences of several layoffs in the company. You may choose to energize the situation by worrying that you may be next or you may choose to protect the peace within your mind. This peace of mind protection is accomplished in two ways. First, stop the channeling of energy to the challenge. Do this by mentally or verbally shouting "Stop." You may wish to visualize a symbol that means stop to you, such as karate chops blocking unwanted types of thinking. Next, repeat these words from *A Course in Miracles*, "I can choose peace instead of this." Picture peace as a white being residing in your mind that you are protecting.

Give yourself a success shower. Sometimes in the business world, other actors insult us, decrease our confidence, or compete with us. It is important that we restore our beliefs that we are one with God and that we dwell in love and have choices. In the silence, get in a peaceful state. Imagine Divine light coming into the top of your head. Raise your hands to touch the Divine light and shower it from your head to other areas in your body. As you shower yourself with the light, know that the light brings absolute love, wisdom, power, serenity, guidance, healing, health, humor, contentment, or zeal to you. You can imagine the shower to be any substance or color — perhaps many sparkling lights or pink droplets. Use your creative energies.

If you are faced with a disappointment such as harsh criticism or a lower pay increase than you expected, find ways to raise your attitude. Find something that will make you happy. Remind yourself of your other successes, and look for affirmations to focus your mind on positive things. Do not allow another business person's words or actions to steal your power and success.

Sometimes our business cards contain a title that does not accurately reflect the full scope of our responsibilities. However, our managers are not willing to give us a more elevated title. Take your business card, white out the title, and print "the Divine Essence" as the title. This title is the greatest title anyone can have. Hold that image in your mind. Recall that image any time you feel sad that your title is less than your responsibilities.

*. . . a mental vibration of impulse. Each thought has an identity that has a central ego, around which all elements revolve. Thoughts are capable of expressing themselves. Every thought clothes itself in a life form according to the character given it by the thinker. The form is simply the conclusion of the thought.*

*Charles Fillmore,* The Revealing Word

*The pleasantest things in the world are pleasant thoughts, and the greatest art in life is to have as many of them as possible.*

*C.N. Buree*

*four*

# PEACEFUL THINKING

Because Wisdom and Wonder were to attend the same meeting the next day, Wisdom made arrangements for them to meet in the conference room before the meeting. The appointment was later than usual, and so Wonder spent a restless morning at this desk. When he finally focused on his work, he found the time went by quickly and pretty soon it was time for him to head up to the corporate conference room on the top floor.

It was an elaborate room with spacious windows overlooking the city in all directions. He arrived a few minutes early and took in the view, the polished mahogany table, and the powerful, thickly upholstered chairs. Sinking down into one of them, he began to review his lessons so far. Sitting there alone and in silence, Wonder pondered the powerful ways in which the mind works.

## THOUGHTS

Wisdom appeared shortly thereafter, and began the conversation as if she had been reading his mind.

"Mind stuff or mental energy originates as neutral energy that we have the power to mold as we choose. This is also known as the ethers. It was defined by Charles Fillmore like this: 'The spiritual substance in which we live, move, and have our being and out of which can be made whatever we desire.'"

"Oh, Hi! I didn't even hear you come in!"

"Well, we don't have much time today, so I thought I'd just jump in. Okay?"

"Sure, but let me catch up. I don't comprehend all this mind stuff, mental energy, or ethers. Could you explain it differently?"

"Let's see . . . Think of mind stuff or mental energy as a large glob of gray clay."

"Okay. I can visualize that."

"This gray clay symbolizing mind stuff is formless. You are the one who creates thoughts by thinking — just as you would mold clay. These thoughts are created from any of your three components — mind, body, or spirit as I already mentioned. Your thoughts can be any shape or size depending upon the intensity and frequency of the energy you are using to mold this clay. Once the creation is completed (the thought is formed), you have a mental object that carries positive or negative energy. It's as if you've created a living effect from the gray blob of mind stuff, and it does have power over you and other people," Wisdom said.

"What you're talking about sounds sort of scary. It makes me realize the seriousness of creating thoughts. Do other people share this viewpoint?"

"Yes, of course. Ralph Waldo Trine summed it up quite well: 'Thoughts are forces . . . They have form, quality, substance, and power.' And Ernest Holmes said, 'According to the sum total of our thoughts, we are either attracting good to us or repelling it from us.' So you see, Wonder, I'm not making this up."

"Obviously the thoughts we create are powerful, and we are responsible for their positive or negative effects. . . . So, if I think back to the actors we saw in the remedial classroom, are you saying that those actors would not be there or could pass out of there if they created their thoughts differently?"

"Why yes, Wonder! William James says it better than I can: 'We are where we are and what we are because of our habitual thinking.' Those corporate actors have habitually created nonproportional thoughts that have out-pictured in the form of fear, hatred, anger, grudges, nonforgiveness, and so on. They have nourished these thoughts repeatedly by giving them energy so the thoughts become strong and constant."

"Okay. I understand that we have the power to create thoughts and to nourish thoughts which then function as forces in our lives that determine where we are and what we are. But what if we did not use good judgment in creating some thoughts? What if we now want some of those thought forces out of our lives?"

"Just because you have created a particular thought doesn't mean it has to remain. The secret is 'change.' Norman Vincent Peale says, 'Change your thoughts and you can change your world.' Scripture also tells us, 'Do not be conformed to this world, but be transformed by the renewing of your mind' (Romans 12:2)."

"Sounds like there's some hope for those actors but how does change happen?"

"In a variety of ways depending upon the type of unproductive thought. They can be grouped into categories and we can change those thoughts by special methods that are geared toward each category. It may sound confusing but think of health and illness. Often, there is a different treatment for each illness. The ultimate goal is to produce health. In our spiritual lives, there is a different treatment for the different types of less than good thoughts. The ultimate goal is to produce productive, peaceful thoughts."

"Okay. Tell me about the different types of less than good thoughts."

"Certainly. Let's first consider the 'stuck thought.'"

STUCK THOUGHTS

"Here's an old Zen story to help illustrate my point:

"Two monks were walking by a river at daybreak in the early spring. Swollen with melted snow, the river coursed above its banks immersing the local footbridge — the only crossing for miles in either direction — under two feet of water. A young woman in a silk dress stood by the riverbank, terrified of the rushing water. Seeing the monks, she flashed them a look of pleading. Without a word, the first monk scooped her up in his arms, held her aloft as he struggled across the submerged bridge, and set her down on the far bank. The two monks then continued walking in silence until sunset, when the vows of their order allowed them to speak.

"'How could you have picked up that woman?' sputtered the second monk, his eyes blazing with anger. 'You know very well that we are prohibited from even thinking about women, let alone touching them. You sullied your honor. You are a disgrace to the whole order.' He shook his fist at his companion.

"'Venerable brother,' said the first monk. 'I put that woman down on the other side of the river at sunrise. It is you who have been carrying her around all day.'"

"So that monk's thoughts were really stuck . . . and on a perceived wrong!" Wonder exclaimed. "Just how do thoughts get stuck? Aren't we always creating new thoughts?"

"Yes, but sometimes our thoughts get stuck, even though new ones are being created. Can you imagine the needle of a phonograph getting stuck on a particular record groove. What's that sound like?"

"Well, it's a repetition of a particular word or note and it's not pleasant to hear. In fact, it's rather disturbing. The needle stays stuck until it is lifted and put on another groove. Then, the listening experience is again harmonious."

"Exactly! The same thing happens with our thoughts. Sometimes when we have an unpleasant experience such as being criticized in public or being treated unjustly, our initial reaction may be to hold a grudge. We may choose not to forgive and think that we can get back at the person who we perceive has harmed us. As we think this way, we replay the unpleasant words or actions. We may even get our thoughts more stuck by reliving the experience as we tell others about the unfair act. Our thoughts are then not free, creative, unlimited, or prosperous — they are stuck."

"So how do we get them unstuck? What is the force that is similar to lifting the phonograph needle from the groove?"

"Glad you asked. The force is forgiveness."

"Yes, I've heard about that but more in a preachy sort of way."

"Preachy? How so?"

"I guess in the way that if you're a good, spiritual person, you should forgive other people."

"Let me expand your understanding of forgiveness. It is not something you do or owe another person for it carries no benefit to another person. Forgiveness is not about condoning and is not about forgetting. Forgiveness is about releasing the painful energy that you have associated in the memory of an action that you have judged to be unfair. Forgiveness is something you do for yourself; it is a gift to yourself!"

"Oh, I see. It allows our thoughts to be unstuck and peaceful."

"Then you can create new and prosperous thoughts."

"I have another question. How do we forgive? Is it a matter of saying, 'I forgive you' and then our thoughts will be unstuck?"

"Hang onto that question and it will be answered as we 'walk the talk.'"

"Okay, I'll be waiting. So what are the other types of thinking that get us stuck?"

ERROR THOUGHTS

"Sometimes we stop ourselves from thinking peaceful thoughts by engaging in 'error thinking.' This type of thinking does not allow us to express our full Divine potential. What do you think these thoughts might be?"

"I suppose they would include any worry or doubtful thinking. Maybe like:

"I don't know if I can do this job for I really don't have very much experience.

"How can I make any sales in this economic climate?

"I'm not smart enough to apply for that advancement.

"How can I survive in the business world when someone with so much clout is challenging me?

"Or what if my sales don't improve?" Wonder offered.

"Super job! All of these are good examples of error thinking. We move from error thinking to peaceful thinking by a process called 'denials and affirmations.'"

"What's that?"

"According to Charles Fillmore, 'Two movements of the mind that express power to accept or to reject, to lay hold of or to let go.'"

Wonder looked puzzled, but Wisdom was quiet and let him ponder the words for a moment.

"So... we must consciously decide... via our minds what we want to let go of or disclaim and what we want to attract into our life in order to achieve success?" Wonder said.

"Exactly. In fact, Og Mandino summarizes Charles Fillmore's words and your words in a slightly different manner: 'Good habits are the key to all success... My bad habits must be destroyed and new furrows prepared for good seed.'"

"Okay, so how do we do it?"

## DENIALS

*He who wishes to follow me, let him deny himself,*
*and take up his cross and follow me.*
*Matthew 16:24*

*The mental process of erasing from consciousness the*
*false beliefs of the sense mind.*
*Charles Fillmore,* The Revealing Word

"With the tool of denials, we stop nourishing or stop giving energy to a thought that we no longer want to have exist. We recognize that thought as a false belief that no longer has power over our good," Wisdom explained to her student, who sat with rapt attention across from her with his hands folded together on his lap.

He thought about her words, looked down at his hands, wiggled a little in his seat and said, "Let me make sure I understand you. We have created a large or small limiting belief that we habitually nourish. We decide to see things differently — to create thoughts differently. However, our error thoughts still exist out there. By denying or refusing to accept their power, the thoughts disappear and are no longer forces in our lives."

Wisdom smiled. He was rapidly becoming one of her best students.

"That is correct. However, nature or the universe will not permit voids to exist in our lives. Thus, when we deny or get rid of a thought force, a replacement thought must fill that void. Rather than attracting the mental energy that has been created by someone else, it is wise to create a productive thought force by using the tool of affirmations."

AFFIRMATIONS

> . . . the mental movement that asserts confidently and persistently the Truth of Being in the face of all appearances to the contrary.
>
> Charles Fillmore, The Revealing Word

> You shall also decree a thing, and it shall be established.
>
> Job 22:28

> Do not be conformed to this world but be you transformed by the renewal of your mind, that you may prove what is the will of God, what is good and acceptable and perfect.
>
> Romans 12:2

"So what does the affirmation do?" Wonder asked, still slightly unclear about the process.

"When we affirm, we consciously create a thought that links us with the Divine part of us or with the 'I am' part of us," Wisdom said, recognizing the understanding in Wonder's eyes.

He stood up and walked toward the window. Placing his hand on his forehead he paused for a minute before continuing.

"I am reminded of something else you have told me . . . that the 'I am' part of us connects us with our Source so that our lives can be perfect. To me, perfection in my life translates to health, wealth, love, happiness. So if the 'I am' inner part of me is perfect in those areas, then is it possible for me to create through my thoughts, the perfect attributes that I affirm?"

"Yes, it is," Wisdom assured Wonder. "Affirmations can be created in two ways. First, an affirmation can begin with the words, 'I am' for those two words link us to our Source and remind us of our perfection. For example, 'I am serene when dealing with irate clients.' Second, an affirmation may simply affirm the positive or the good in a situation, such as 'I utilize infinite intelligence and wisdom when making decisions for my company.'

"Wonder, it is important to remember that denials and affirmations are not magic words or magical spells. The particular words chosen are not that important. Denials and affirmations simply help us to remove false beliefs and to create true beliefs. What is very important is the feelings or vibrations that are produced from denying and affirming."

"So it seems that certain thoughts are addictive, and we need to free ourselves from them. How do I do that?" Wonder inquired.

## ADDICTIVE THOUGHTS

"Excellent observation. Ken Keyes has a great definition about that: 'Life is warning you to get rid of an addiction every time you are emotionally uncomfortable in any way.' I realize that's a rather bold statement, but let's play for awhile to see how we feel about it."

Wonder was ready to rebut the words. He was eager to share his ideas. He turned and took a subtly aggressive pose. Wisdom smiled inwardly sensing his newfound strength. *This is good,* she thought. *He needs to build some confidence.* She listened.

"I don't think of emotions in relation to addictions, but rather in relation to smoking, drinking, drugs, food, that sort of thing. It's odd to think that our addictions are causing us to feel uncomfortable rather than the people doing the actions."

"Well, you'll see the connection in a minute. What I'd like you to do, Wonder, is to think of some work situations that have made you or other actors uncomfortable and then share how addictions might be present."

"Okay.

"I feel angry when my boss is authoritative, so . . . I have an addiction to want to share in the decision making process.

"I feel sad and envious when some employees in my company are groomed and coddled while other employees are ignored, so . . . I have an addiction to fairness.

"I feel angry and envious when some co-workers in my company earn more than others in the same capacity, so . . . again I have an addiction to fairness.

"I feel hurt when I work overtime or do outside projects and I am not praised or compensated, so . . . I have an addiction for outer appreciation.

"I feel angry and anxious when I am waiting for my boss or clients to call me back at a designated time but it doesn't happen, so . . . I have an addiction to wanting people to keep their word.

"I feel hurt when my boss or clients use an argumentative tone with their voice mail messages, so . . . I have an addiction to wanting people to speak politely to me.

"I feel angry when my boss won't recognize my overtime contributions, so . . . I have an addiction to wanting people to appreciate my efforts."

"Boy, that's really claiming responsibility. You have really understood how addictions cause us anger, hurt, unhappiness, and all those other emotions. How did you feel about making that claim, Wonder?"

"Well, it made me realize that I do have power over my feelings and that the other actors and I do have some addictive thoughts that can be changed to peaceful thinking, but how?"

"The key to changing addictions to peaceful thinking is through changing the addictions to preferences. When we have only the 'preference' that something happens or that someone does or does not do something, we remove emotional energy from the person or from the situation. Therefore, if the outcome is not what we had expected, we are still at peace. So, having preferences instead of addictions is the key to happiness. Addictions keep us from having peaceful thinking and from experiencing our good for we are occupied with such discomfort that we cannot concentrate on our greater good or on the all-ness of God."

"So addictions are sort of like attachments, and preferences are just ideas that we can easily adapt as the situations needs? Is that it?"

"That's it!"

"So how do I do it?"

## Walking the Talk

"Here's a very practical exercise that can set the tone for thoughts throughout the day and during sleep. Just as we brush our teeth in the morning and the evening, so can we brush our thoughts.

"In a meditative state, image Divine light entering your head area. Ask that this Divine light purify your thoughts. Visualize the light swishing through your head. For each negative thought, see this strong, white light brushing the thought, brushing the negativity of it. It cleanses the negative thought and a positive thought remains. Conclude by visualizing yourself filled with Divine wisdom and guidance. This exercise can be a tool for helping you avoid negative thoughts and judgments."

Wonder relaxed for a moment, visualizing this calming meditation. He liked it and vowed to start using it every day.

Knowing they were pressed for time, Wisdom glanced at her watch. She would have loved to let Wonder stay in his meditation, but she knew before long the room would be flooded with co-workers.

"Let's consider unsticking our thoughts via forgiveness. You are right about forgiveness, Wonder — it is easier said than done. As a first step, you must develop ways to stop the mind from dwelling on the injustice. I'll share some ways that you might wish to adopt. First, from *A Course in Miracles*, you could use the phrase I have already mentioned, 'I can choose peace instead of this.'"

"So when we're reliving the pain of a situation, we can remind ourselves that we have the power of choosing peace instead of choosing pain?"

"Yes. Another helpful idea from *A Course in Miracles* is, 'This instant is the only time there is.'"

"How many times I've heard that!" Wonder said with a great deal of exasperation. Wisdom could see that as with most people, living in the present was a difficult task for him.

"Sometimes it is easier to use imagery. Imagine a large, white raft labeled 'PEACE OF MIND.' Picture your mind clinging to the raft."

"And that will help me forgive and let go of negative thoughts?"

"That's *part* of the forgiveness process," Wisdom cautioned.

"And the rest?"

"First you let go of the pain associated with the experience (though not necessarily the experience itself) that tries persistently to repeat itself in your mind. The other part of the forgiveness process is to let go of any negative emotion you may feel whenever you think of, see, or interact with the person who created that experience."

"How does that happen?"

"Several ways. First, consider Martin Luther King's response to the commandment of loving our enemies. He said: 'Forgiveness does not mean ignoring what has been done or putting a false label on an evil act. It means, rather, that the evil act no longer remains as a barrier to the relationship . . . We must recognize that the evil deed of the enemy neighbor, the thing that hurts, never quite expresses all that he is. An element of goodness may be found even in our worst enemy.'

"So, dear Wonder, the answer to your question is to love the other person we feel may have harmed us by recognizing the good, the indwelling God, within them."

Wonder was quiet. He knew of some people in whom he would have tremendous difficulty recognizing the indwelling God, but he would give it a try. He was anxious to know how he might do that.

"Okay, now can you tell me some practical ways to get rid of error thinking?"

"Sure. But first I'd like to reference a biblical verse: 'If there is faith in you even as a grain of mustard seed, you will say to this mountain, "move away from here, and it will move away; and nothing would prevail over you"' (Matthew 17:20). Actors can use the denial portion of this verse by saying to a challenging work situation: 'Move away from here for you have no power over me.' The affirmation portion of this can be in the words, 'I now attract the highest and best work situation for all concerned.'"

Then Wisdom reached in her briefcase. Wonder knew that another treasure was forthcoming. He had already started a notebook for his own notes and for all the lists and handouts that Wisdom presented him with. It was becoming a wonderful reference tool.

"Here, Wonder, are some other denial and affirmation combinations for you to look over later."

Wonder began to read the list.

My good cannot be limited; my career fulfillment cannot be blocked. I move forward

through the pain to receive my highest good.

I deny the power of age discrimination. I know that my good cannot be withheld. I attract my abundant rewards as I lovingly share my time and knowledge with my employer.

The tone and sarcasm from my employee has no effect upon me. I will not allow her words to disturb my peace of mind. I am powerful, loving, stable, and serene in all of my interactions with her. I salute the indwelling God within her. Amen.

The economic condition has no effect upon my sales. I know that the Divine within me is absolute financial abundance. Through the power of the Divine, I attract clients who quickly and eagerly purchase my products. I affirm that my products provide my clients with quality and my clients provide my company with increased prosperity. Blessings to all.

This challenging work situation ends quickly and in peace for all concerned. I lovingly release the current situation and the current situation lovingly releases me. I move to my highest and best place of employment where I am happy with the responsibilities, salary, commission, environment, recognition, management, and employees. And so it is. Amen.

I refuse to accept any type of limitations

in my life. There is no lack in my life. There is no lack of time in my life. I call on the divine power of organization, wisdom, and action to accomplish all tasks before me. All my projects begin and end with God. Amen.

My manager has no power over my peace of mind. I am strong and I am unaffected by his words.

I deny any beliefs in fear of disharmony. The performance review I conduct is filled with absolute love and harmony. I utilize divine wisdom to judge with right judgment rather than from appearances. I share feedback with my employee in a loving, caring manner. My employee and I move forward to create improvements that benefit our organization. And so it is.

I deny any appearance of a lack in qualified personnel. I quickly attract more qualified personnel who are in a salary range that complements my company's budget.

As Wonder looked over the paper, Wisdom added, "There is a slightly amusing little system worked out by Jose Silva and Ed Bernd in their book, *Sales Power: The Silva Mind Method for Sales Professionals*. When doubts or negative thoughts occur, you can mentally or verbally say 'Cancel-Cancel' and can then affirm 'Better-and-Better.'

"When I used this denial/affirmation aid, Wonder, I found it helpful to repeat my denials and affirmations. During some difficult testing periods of my soul, I wrote my denials and affirmations over and over on a piece of paper. Sometimes I had to do this in the little gaps in my schedule such as when I was early for a client's meeting. I even wrote denials and affirmations in the car!"

Wonder laughed. He imagined himself scribbling affirmations in strange places: standing in line at the bank, riding in an elevator. He was beginning to notice how many opportunities there were for such activities.

"There's also a method for someone who likes to be very organized. Write the affirmations on index cards. These index cards can be inserted in the plastic sleeves of a mini photo album. You can look at them first thing in the morning as well as throughout the day."

"I'm not sure I'm that organized," Wonder laughed. "Before we end, could you give me an idea of how to change addictions into preferences?"

"Sure, this is a fun one. First, get in the habit of changing your words. Let's think back to some of your addictions. I'll show you how the wording might be changed. For example, instead of saying, 'I want you to leave me polite voice mail messages and to return my calls when you say you will,' you might instead say, 'I prefer that you leave me polite voice mail messages and I prefer that you return my calls when you say you will.' Get in the habit of using statements with the word *prefer*," Wisdom explained.

"Such a minute change but it sure makes a difference since our mind hears and interprets our spoken word. Is the method of changing addictions to preferences as easy as just stating that we have preferences?"

Wisdom was enjoying their conversation. His observation pleased her. Although she still thought of herself as an advisor, she noticed Wonder's willingness to extend himself and to engage his brain in matters that were difficult and confusing. She respected him for this, and as a result they began to feel more like peers than student and teacher.

"No, not quite, Wonder. In addition to using preferences in our words, we might also elicit preferences in our feelings. We do that by being sensitive to our feelings. Whenever we feel anxious or like we're attaching some of our feelings to a person or situation and their outcome, we can use some self-talk like this: 'I deny the external power I've been giving to the outcome of this situation. I choose to channel that power to my indwelling God. I prefer that the outcome is (blank line) but I trust that all things work through God for good.

"Or, sometimes, we may feel like our power is being drawn from us to the situation with a particular outcome that we're trying to force to happen. In this particular situation, we might shake out our hands and legs and repeat, 'I relax and prefer that (blank line) happens.' This can be repeated several times so that we come to remind ourselves that this is indeed a preference.

"There may not be time to prepare to stop the addiction and move it to a preference. Sometimes an actor will say something or some event will happen that we didn't expect and we may immediately feel angry or hurt. In that case, we can begin by recognizing that we are experiencing an addiction. As a practice exercise (even though it's after the fact), get in a relaxed state. In your mind, visualize yourself handling that very situation from a preference standpoint rather than from an addiction standpoint. This practice is helpful because the more times you practice changing your addictions to preferences, the easier it will be to do so spontaneously."

Barely had the words tumbled from Wisdom's mouth when the double oak-paneled conference room doors swung open and the executive vice president walked in. He stopped for a moment and smiled at the two early birds.

A bonus, Wonder thought, to Wisdom's spiritual lessons. Wonder returned the man's smile and turned briefly to Wisdom.

"Thank you," he whispered. "I really feel I'm on the road to peaceful thinking. It sure will come in handy with some of the teachers I have. So many of them have been really pushing my addiction buttons."

"You're welcome," Wisdom said as she rose to meet the executive vice president.

"A new one you've taken under your wing?" he said with a quiet gleam in his eye.

"You're not my only protégé," she said, taking his arm and walking with him over to the window, where they were soon lost in conversation.

BIBLIOGRAPHY

Borysenko, Joan. *Minding the Body, Mending the Mind.* Reading Mass.: Addison-Wesley Publishing Co., 1987.

Fillmore, Charles. *The Revealing Word.* Unity Village, Mo.: Unity Books, 1988.

Keyes, Ken. *Pathbook to Higher Consciousness.* New York: Living Love Publications, 1975.

Mandino, Og. *The Greatest Salesman in the World.* New York: Bantam Books, 1988.

*. . . Love is not primarily a relationship to a specific person, it is an attitude, an orientation of character which determines the relatedness of a person to the world as a whole, not toward one 'object of love.'*

*Erich Fromm,* The Art of Loving

*There is no difficulty that love will not conquer; no disease that enough love will not heal; no door that enough love will not open; no gulf that enough love will not bridge; no wall that enough love will not throw down; no sin that enough love will not redeem... It makes no difference how deeply seated may be the trouble; how hopeless the outlook; how muddled the tangle; how great the mistake. A sufficient realization of love will dissolve it all. If only you could love enough you would be the happiest and most powerful being in the world.*

*Emmet Fox,* The Sermon on the Mount

*Love is patient, love is kind, and is not jealous; love does not brag and is not arrogant, does not take into account a wrong suffered, does not rejoice in unrighteousness, but rejoices with the truth; bears all things, believes all things, hopes all things, endures all things.*

(Corinthians 13:4-8)

*five*

# LOVE

Wisdom had a meeting out of the office, so she asked Wonder to meet her at an outdoor restaurant downtown. Wonder arranged to use some of his overtime to take a little extra time at lunch so they wouldn't be rushed. As Wonder stepped outside, he breathed in the warm air and felt the cool spring sun settle on his skin. He decided to walk and arrived at the restaurant just as Wisdom was departing a cab.

"Hello! So what are today's lessons?" he asked.

"Today," Wisdom said as she steered him into the restaurant, "we are going to discuss love."

Of course, just as Wisdom said "love," the maître d' appeared and smiled as if the two were lovers. Wonder blushed, and Wisdom just returned the smile as if nothing could be more natural. As a result, he escorted them to a secluded and quiet nook of the atrium, where they could converse in relative privacy.

"There are sometimes benefits to misunderstandings," Wisdom said.

"So what does love have to do with getting ahead in business, which I normally see as a cold, calculating sort of process?"

"Love is a very strong aid. But this type of love is different from the romantic type of love. It's also different from the family or obligatory kind."

While folding and refolding his napkin, Wonder recalled feeling obligated to love certain family members because it was the right thing to do. He was relieved that he did not have to do that in the business world. Although Wisdom wasn't obligating him to love other associates, she was proposing that he do it naturally, but he really didn't understand how.

"But how can you naturally love someone when their actions are wrong or harmful to others?"

"We do not have to like or agree with someone's actions. However, we can still love that person. When we love other people, we are not necessarily loving their behavior. Rather, we are loving the spiritual, divine part of them."

"That advice sounds familiar. Isn't there a story about ducks or eagles or something?" Wonder asked while trying to get another peek at the menu before Wisdom answered.

"Yes! But it was seagulls. *Jonathan Livingston Seagull.* If you remember, Jonathan had been banished by his flock and experienced many hardships. Another seagull, Fletcher, spoke to Jonathan and said, 'I don't understand how you manage to love a mob of birds that has just tried to kill you.' Jonathan replied, 'Oh Fletch, you don't love that! You don't love hatred and evil, of course. You have to practice and see the real gull, the good in every one of them, and to help them see it in themselves. That's what I mean by love. It's fun, when you get the knack of it.'"

Recalling the backstabbing, the competitiveness, and the dishonesty on his team, Wonder doubted the process of love could be fun. Contemplating that the team's actions were not what each member was really like, he asked, "So seeing the 'real gull' is like seeing the Divine part in other people?"

"Exactly. I think it was Eric Fromm who wrote, 'If I perceive in another person mainly the surface, I perceive mainly the differences, that which separates us. If I penetrate to the core, I perceive our identity, the fact of our brotherhood.'"

Wonder's thoughts penetrated past the faces of his team, past their actions. "So love means going past the outer, physical part of a person and focusing on the inner, invisible, spiritual part of a person."

"You're right on target," Wisdom interrupted. She in turn was interrupted by a large-eyed, grandfatherly waiter who reached over and lit the candle on their table.

"May your lives be blessed with a passionate and bright love like the light of this flame." He then proceeded to take their order.

Wonder blushed, gave the waiter his order, and when the man took Wisdom's and left, Wonder looked down at the table.

"Um . . . Do you want me to blow out the candle?" he whispered.

Wisdom laughed lightly as she marveled at yet another joke from the universe. A tear slipped down her cheek, but she didn't say anything so the candle stayed lit. She continued her explanations.


FEAR

> *Fear always distorts our perceptions and confuses us as to what is going on . . . Although Love is always what we really want, we are often afraid of Love without consciously knowing it, and so we may act both blind and deaf to Love's presence. Yet, as we help ourselves and each other let go of fear, we begin to experience a personal transformation. We start to see beyond our old reality as defined by the physical senses, and we enter a state of clarity in which we discover that all minds are joined, that we share a common Self, and that inner peace and Love are in fact all that are real . . . Love, then, is letting go of fear."*
> *Gerald Jampolsky, M.D.,*
> Love Is Letting Go of Fear

Wonder was trying to digest the idea of loving someone who had not behaved properly. He recalled a manager who had purposely withheld a promotion from him.

"What about those people in business situations who intentionally hurt us?"

"Remember the story I told you about how I tried to make special gifts for my boss when we had scheduled meetings, only to be stood up or ignored. I did it because I thought I was extending care and love. However, my actions were not appreciated."

"I have this image, Wisdom," Wonder said. "You were trying to extend unconditional love, say in the form of a lemon meringue pie and someone lifts your own hand with the pie into your own face!"

"Exactly, Wonder. After many lessons, I learned I didn't need pie in my face — that I could offer the pie to people who would accept it. Please understand that I did not turn off unconditional love. Rather, it's like a water hose. The water can be turned on in the pipes (the unconditional love), but it doesn't always have to be spraying from the nozzle. I now wait until someone chooses to turn on the nozzle (accept the unconditional love). Jesus taught this lesson very wisely when he said, 'Whoever will not welcome you and will not listen to your words, when you leave the house of the village, shake off the sand from your feet' (Mat 10:14)."

"Okay," Wonder said, "that's one example, and maybe that guy was unintentionally not responding. But what about people who purposely lash out or treat employees or co-workers badly?"

"You know, Jesus gave us some wise words about challenges. He said, 'But if anyone strikes you on the right cheek, turn the other also' (Matthew 5:39). This means that even though business people may intentionally hurt us, we can turn our cheek away from that pain by seeing things in a different way — in a nonpainful way."

"I suppose," Wonder mused, still not looking convinced.

"Consider this, Wonder. Gerald Jampolsky tells us 'No one attacks unless he first feels threatened and believes that through attack he can demonstrate his own strength, at the expense of another's vulnerability... We are always expressing either love or fear. Fear is really a call for help, and therefore a request for Love.' So, Wonder, these people are acting in fear which is being translated as jealousy, anxiety, aggression. Their actions are being translated by you as being unloving actions. However, love is exactly what their souls *need* to receive from you," explained Wisdom.

Sensing a barrier, Wisdom decided to try again. She knew the mind understands and remembers best that which is absurd, gross, or sexual. She embarked on a different approach.

"You might also want to think of these people coming to you for a healing. Consider a baby with diaper rash. That painful condition is unpleasant in appearance for the baby's bottom may be reddened and blistered. However, it is important for a baby's bottom to be exposed to the air and to receive ointment so that healing occurs. Similarly, some people's inner lives are painful and unpleasant in appearance. Yet, they expose their inner lives (jealousy, selfishness, quick temper, dishonesty, prejudices, and the like) so that you see them and apply an ointment of love. These people come to you for healing because they sense that you are willing to share your love. You might even visualize these people wearing a sweatshirt that has these words printed on it 'Please love me; heal me.'"

*Yikes!* Wonder thought. Last Friday he had baby-sat his sister's daughter, and he recalled how proper looking his niece was in her velvet dress, lace collar, patent leather shoes, and beribboned hair. What an eye opener... and a nose opener! He had to change her diaper, and after clearing up the mess, his breathing momentarily stopped when seeing the reddened skin and blisters on her bottom cheeks. At that time, he had hoped ointment would bring relief.

*How could Wisdom be so right on with this analogy?* he thought. He knew it was a valid one, yet it seemed odd and uncomfortable.

"It's rather unusual to think that the business people who are most challenging to me are the ones who are in most need of my love," he finally said.

"But that's the way it works!"

## PROCRUSTEANISM

> *Love does not consist in gazing at each other but in looking outward together in the same direction.*
> Antoine de Saint-Exupéry

"I now understand the power of love. I understand that business people who are most afraid of us may act in the most unloving manner. However, some of the people I encounter are at the extreme. They are too lazy, too insensitive, too power hungry, too stingy . . . You know what I mean."

"Extremes can be very frustrating. Before our meal arrives, let me share a myth with you. Once upon a time, there lived a Greek king, Procrustes. He hosted dinner parties and invited his guests to stay overnight. His overnight guests were required to sleep in the Procrustean Bed. Procrustes insisted that his guests fit exactly. Thus, if guests were too short, Procrustes would stretch his guests. If his guests were too long, Procrustes would chop off their legs. From this myth, the term 'procrusteanism' has emerged to describe us whenever we insist that someone's characteristics fit exactly to our expectations. When I hear that you'd like to shorten someone's desire for power or that you'd like to lengthen someone's generosity, ambition, or sensitivity, I am hearing you say that you'd like to make them fit the boundaries that you have established for them."

"Weeell yes," Wonder said slowly, using the image of Procrustes as a new way of looking at an activity he normally took for granted.

"I understand that it may be difficult to love someone who does not fit within your boundaries. However, there are productive ways to love people while still respecting their differences. I'll be sharing those ways when we 'walk the talk.' For now let's eat," Wisdom said as she saw the waiter's approach.

"Tuna salad for the striking Romeo and a double garden salad for the ever-enchanting Juliet. Bon appétit," he said winking and gracefully bowing.

## MENTAL AH-SOING

As the plates were cleared and the herbal tea poured, Wonder decided to ask Wisdom about a current personal situation.

"There's a manager who always opposes me. No matter what I do, he finds fault with it. Shouldn't I at least stand up for myself when I know I'm right?"

Wisdom sensed that Wonder was reticent to let anyone get the upper hand. She watched him for a moment while she removed the teabag from the steaming hot water. She sipped the tea, enjoying its warm lemony taste.

"Wonder, in many cases, you will be able to arrive at a win-win situation in which both of your viewpoints are respected and a negotiation process can occur. However, there are times when that approach just isn't possible, so you have to resort to some mental ah-soing."

"So what's that? Sounds Oriental."

"Ken Keyes talks about this concept in his book *Handbook to Higher Consciousness.* He tells the story of a Zen master who had a beautiful young lady as his pupil. She became pregnant, and she falsely named her teacher as the father of her child. When the child was born, her family indignantly brought the child to the Zen master and accused him of taking advantage of his beautiful young pupil. His only reply was, 'Ah-so.' They left the child with the Zen master, who enjoyed caring for it and had many beautiful hours playing with the child. After about a year the young lady was very ill, and not wanting to die with this false accusation on her conscience, she told her family that the real father was a young man who lived in a nearby town. Her mother and father immediately went to the teacher and profoundly bowed and apologized and asked for the baby back. The Zen master gave them the baby and said, 'Ah-so.'

"Wonder, notice that in this story, the Zen master chose to say *ah-so* because the parents were extremely adverse to him and would not have believed his story over their daughter's story. Also, when the parents returned, the Zen did not choose to chastise them; an *ah-so* reply was enough for the Zen master was able to love them. So Wonder, in your dealings with people, you must sometimes weigh if it is more important to be loved or to be right. Please understand that I am a firm believer in being assertive and loving when the conditions warrant that."

"Ah-so," Wonder replied to Wisdom aloud and silently to his manager.

The curious waiter appeared again, and put the check down between them. He looked at Wonder, inclined his head toward Wisdom and winked again. "Enjoy love! Celebrate love," he whispered and then wandered back toward the kitchen.

WALKING THE TALK

> *Whatever your problem, it is but a test in love. If*
> *you meet that test through love, your problem will*
> *be solved. If you do not meet that test through love,*

*your problem will assail you until you do! Your problem is your initiation in love.*
    Catherine Ponder, The Prospering Power of Love

*Love cures people — both the ones who give it and the ones who receive it.*
                 *Dr. Karl Menninger*

Wonder blushed again. "Oh let's get out of here," he said rising quickly and heading toward the door. Wisdom looked at the bill, left the appropriate amount, and rose as well. They walked outside to look for a cab. But Wisdom hesitated.

"It's such an inviting day, why don't we walk back to the office and talk on the way? I'd like to give you some practical ways to deal with these situations."

"Fine, but before you share your ideas, I'd like to give you some more examples of what I deal with and what some of my co-workers go through, Wonder said."

"Yes, of course! I'd be interested in hearing some of the specifics so I can relate practical advice to you," Wisdom responded.

"Okay, consider the following:

> "How do you love a manager who daily insults or power whips employees who then react in tears, rage, or illness?

> "How do you love a manager who lives a life of fakery, who listens to conversations to absorb jargon and then uses that jargon in his speech? He acts just the right way in front of the right people and then goes back to his old ways when they are gone.

"How do you love a manager who brags that he has five buzz words he uses to impress people so they don't question his ability? And you are reviewed by him on an ability level.

"How do you love a manager who spends ninety-five percent of her time socializing or talking on the phone when management isn't around? You are reviewed on an ethical level by her.

"How do you love a manager who discusses confidential concerns with her friends inside and outside of our company? She does our performance review and salary review.

"How do you love a manager who yells at you in front of other employees?

"How do you love a manager who continuously gives promotions to less qualified employees?

"How do you love a manager who comes into work in the morning and smells like alcohol?

"How do you love a manager who times every minute of our breaks and lunches yet sneaks out early in the afternoon for fake appointments?

"How do you love a manager who delegates work he does not know how to do but then takes total credit for it."

"Well, I think that's a pretty good list," Wisdom smiled.

## HOW DO I LOVE THEE?

"Wonder, as you've seen, managers are chosen to be marvelous teachers of love to our souls. Managers have been given great power to control our outer place of employment and sometimes that power can be misused. That misuse of power often triggers a love lesson. We can choose to master it or we can choose to become bitter or angry. So as we walk along here, let's 'walk the talk,'" Wisdom said as she pulled a daisy from a flower bed along the sidewalk.

"How do I love thee, teacher-manager? Let me count the ways." They both laughed.

"Okay, she continued, "Here are some examples. You might say:

"I can realize that you, dear manager, are doing the absolute best job you can do at this particular time. You simply do not know any better way to act.

"I can replace each disturbing image by my own positive image. When you discuss my salary with your friends, I can image musical notes of love coming from your mouth. When you rearrange your desk to look busy before our boss enters the room, I can image love and light emitting from your desk. When you insult other employees, I can image those same musical notes of love coming from your mouth.

"I can hold in mind the image of you as you are outside of work — the loving way you react with your family at social functions, the joy on your face as you slide down the water slide at a company picnic. I'll see you that way when I view you at work.

"I will remember that you are calling to me for a healing. I will image you wearing a company tee shirt that says, 'Please love me; please heal me.'

"I will practice to see the 'real gull' in you. Thus, I will silently speak, 'I behold the Divine in you.' I will also silently speak to you the word *namaste,* which means the 'Divinity in me salutes the Divinity in you.'

"I will try to see your actions in a positive manner. For example, if you talk loudly, I will view you as being assertive rather than bossy.

"I will act like a detective for I will daily search and list the good I catch you doing or being.

"I will communicate to your angel, soul, and Higher Self, a subject we will discuss in detail sometime soon.

"I will utilize an idea from Og Mandino who writes, 'And how will I confront each whom I meet? In only one way. In silence and to myself I will address him and say I love you.' So for you, dear manager, I will silently say, 'I love you' when I see you and when I think about you.

"I will practice releasing or creating a vacuum so that love will have room to expand. I will release hatred, anger, and nonforgiveness. Also, in time, I will release you and you will release me."

Wisdom tossed the spent daisy into the grass and glanced at her student, who looked more than sated with information.

"Sheesh. That's a lot to remember and a lot to think about. I'd rather have our next lesson in two days instead of tomorrow," Wonder said breathlessly not from the walk but from the sheer amount of information Wisdom offered.

"As it should be, Wonder. I'll be out of town tomorrow! And you look as though you could use a little rest from your studies. I've written down the ideas I just mentioned plus some additional ones that you might wish to study as well."

She once again handed him a neatly typed list.

Love Additives

> If you are a salesman, get in the habit of hugging your proposals and mass mailings before you send them out. This is a nice way to send love to the recipient. And, of course, we all know about the law of cause and effect so something great is going to come back to us.

> Quietly speak words such as *love, love, love* as you pass by a challenging business person's office or building. The energy vibration from this spoken word is very strong, so use it.

> If you are at a meeting in a conference room and a particular business person is in the 'hot seat,' send love to him so that he will be protected and calm.

> When you are at a meeting or at a sales call, unobtrusively open your hands (palm up) in your lap and think of love extending from them. This is especially important on your first meeting with someone; you share your blessings to set the tone for positive events and to be open to whatever may happen in that meeting.

Visit people who are losing their jobs. Project your inner love during your interactions so that they might have strength and be led to their True Place.

If you receive a stressful memo, before discussing it with the author, be sure to bless the memo. Literally, give it a hug and send it love energy. Many times by just that action, the words on the memo will be nullified and the memo will be positively revised or canceled without any discussion or negotiation.

They arrived at their office building and rode up in the elevator together, Wonder exiting on the fifth floor. Wonder went directly to his office and placed the new addition to his lessons in the special ring binder he had set up. Within minutes, his manager was by his side. He had obviously forgotten that Wonder had used his overtime for a long lunch.

"A little late from lunch, young man. I have to finish the initial report on the Porter-Moss merger, but I have a dental appointment. I want you to finish it. You can sign my name, then send it up to Walters," he said abruptly as he walked out the door.

"Namaste, Namaste," Wonder whispered.

BIBLIOGRAPHY

Bach, Richard. *Jonathan Livingston Seagull.* New York: Avon Books, 1970.

Fromm, Eric. *The Art of Loving.* New York: Harper & Row, 1956.

Jampolsky, Gerald. *Love is Letting Go of Fear.* Berkeley, Ca.: Celestial Arts, 1979.

Keyes, Ken. *Handbook to Higher Consciousness.* New York: Living Love Publications, 1975.

Mandino, Og. *The Greatest Salesman in the World.* New York: Bantam Books, 1988.

*Now faith is the assurance of things hoped for.*

Heb. 11:1

*Faith is the habitual center of man's personal energies.*

*William James*

*Faith is the bird that feels the light, and sings while the dawn is still dark.*

*Anonymous*

*If there is faith in you even as a grain of mustard seed, you will say to this mountain, move away from here, and it will move away; and nothing should prevail over you.*

Matt. 17:20

*six*

# FAITH

Wonder found that his work was going along smoother. On the day Wisdom was out of town, he sailed through the stacks on his desk and he had a little extra time to review the tools she had presented to him.

He received an email message from Wisdom on the morning of her return, suggesting that they meet at their usual time in her office. Wonder had been doing a lot of thinking and he was eager to ask some questions, especially about faith — a new word in his equally new "spiritual" vocabulary.

As was their custom, they spent a few minutes in silence before beginning their conversation.

"So," Wisdom asked quietly, "what have you been doing these last few days?"

"I've been thinking about faith. I perceive, for some reason, it is a powerful study aid in this school for the soul, but it seems rather vague to me; it is just a word."

As Wonder spoke, Wisdom recalled her previous students. "Many people feel as you do, Wonder. That is why faith is probably the least used study aid. However, during our discussion today, we'll explore the five components of faith. Then I think you'll have fun using it."

Rubbing his chin and then flipping to a clean page in his notebook, Wonder said, "I didn't know there were components to faith."

## Desire

"The first component necessary for faith to exist is *desire*. There are two flavors of desire. Some desires are light like wishes. Other desires are very deep rooted and are called *heart's desires*."

"Let's see, I remember a quote you shared with me about heart's desire. You know the one from Emmet Fox. It's here somewhere," he said flipping through his notebook. "Ah, here it is."

Wonder read it aloud:

> "Already in your past life from time to time, God Himself has whispered into your heart just that very wonderful thing, whatever it is, that He is wishing you to be, and to do, and to have. And that wonderful thing is nothing less than what is called your Heart's Desire. Nothing less than that. The most secret, sacred wish that lies deep down at the bottom of your heart, the wonderful thing that you hardly dare to look at, or to think about — the thing that you would rather die than have anyone else know of, because it seems to be so far beyond anything that you are, or have at the present time, that you fear that you would be cruelly ridiculed if the mere thought of it were known — that is the very thing that God is wishing for you to do or to be for Him. And the birth of that marvelous wish in your soul — the dawning of that secret dream — was the Voice of God Himself telling you to arise and come up higher because He has need of you."

"Wonder, I'm impressed that you study and remember and use all the information we discuss," Wisdom praised him.

"I've especially enjoyed that definition of a heart's desire. And just between us," he whispered shyly, "you know, my eyes tend to tear up when I read it. Thanks."

Wisdom shared an empathetic smile as she recalled this, too, was one of her "tissue-requiring" passages. "Wonder, I don't really know if I explained that desire literally means 'of the Father.' And a side note here: please understand that 'of the Father' is not meant to be gender specific so you may think of it as male, female, or neutral.

"Anyway, a desire for something, someone, or some condition is created by God. A desire, then, is like a strong wish that becomes invisibly embedded in our bodies. We may try to forget about a desire or wish that the desire would go away, but it is permanent."

"Let me stop you a moment. If a desire is from our Father, why would we want to forget that desire or wish that it would go away?"

Wisdom noticed Wonder's naiveté and she hoped her explanation would provide thorough preparation for the "desire" test.

"Ah, yes. There's one small point I didn't mention. Although desires are really wonderful and are 'of the Father,' desires are often very difficult to achieve — especially heart's desires."

"Now I feel really confused. If desires are 'of the Father,' why doesn't the Father let our desires be easily achieved?"

While Wisdom answered, Wonder reached into a candy dish on her desk. *She must have replenished the supply this morning. Time for a sugar break to soothe my nerves,* he thought. *Toffee vanilla cream should do the trick.* Wisdom's voice floated sweetly to his ears as he felt the candy melt in his mouth.

"The Father knows that desires are permanent and internal. He knows that we would feel uncomfortable if the desires were not achieved. Therefore, the Father presents different challenges to us for He knows that we must conquer those challenges in order to pursue our desires so that we might be happy. The result of conquering challenges is the Father's goal — the spiritual evolution of our souls as we acquire different virtues and evolve to the perfection of God," Wisdom explained.

"I've known people who have desires but who seem to be confronted with one severe challenge after another, which blocks their desires from happening. And those desires seem to be dearer than life itself to those people. But I also see people who easily achieve those same goals and those goals mean very little to those people. Now I understand which goals are wishes and which goals are heart's desires," Wonder offered.

"Insightful observation, Wonder! Quite often, you may see someone who has a heart's desire (say, to be a manager, marketing rep, anchor person, minister — whatever their choice) who is confronted by challenges that seem to block that desire from manifesting. Yet you'll also see managers, marketing reps, anchor persons, ministers who easily received their jobs, who may poorly perform their jobs, or who may dislike their jobs for the desire was never really there."

"Oh, I've seen plenty of those," Wonder recalled.

"By the way, Wonder, when people do eventually achieve their heart's desire by conquering challenges, they are often outstanding because they perform through the Father and because they have evolved spiritually. In other words, they have performed their pre-desire jobs from their heart with the focus on God."

"Sometimes it seems as if we can never achieve our desires," Wonder mourned.

"Sometimes we cannot. But there are lessons to be learned from this too. Even short-term desires can teach us lessons. For instance, there was an outstanding gentleman who worked for the same company that I did but in another state. He had a comprehensive understanding of what is necessary to accomplish successful business mergers in the human relations department. Once the financial and tax teams are finished, you know how important it is to facilitate communications between the two companies and create smooth transition plans."

"Of course," Wonder nodded.

"I spoke to him over the phone on several occasions and finally I asked him if I might participate on one of his merger teams to learn more about combining work forces and management. He was flattered and agreed to inform me when he had a situation where it would be appropriate for me to be involved. He found one, and I asked my boss if I might take off a day and make up that time by working additional hours."

"Sounds reasonable. You'd be making yourself more valuable to the company and even work overtime to achieve this."

"Well, it was not a reasonable request to my manager. He bellowed at me and those around, 'Contrary to what people might think, I'm still manager and people aren't going to do what they want to do.'

"I continued to nourish my desire to facilitate the efficient and harmonious blending of employee teams, but it seemed I was stuck in the role of helping others implement their plans."

"Did you ever get to observe the manager you admired?"

"No. He retired and moved far away by the time I became a transition specialist."

"And what have you possibly learned in having your desire denied and being humiliated in front of your peers?"

"Quite a few lessons, Wonder. First, I learned a lot about patience. I learned how to coddle, nourish, and protect my desire so it would be strong and good when it was eventually released. Last, from the humiliation, I learned a lot about reacting and responding and that I was responsible for how I was feeling."

Wonder thought about this carefully. It made sense, but he wished there were an answer to how long a pre-desire job lasted. He knew Wisdom couldn't possibly know because it must be different for each person. He'd just have to figure it out for himself.

BELIEF

> *What a man accomplishes depends on what he*
> *believes.*
>
> *Bankers Bulletin*

> *To accomplish great things, we must not only act but*
> *also dream, not only plan but also believe.*
>
> *Anatole France*

> *Believe you have it, and you have it.*
>
> *Latin Proverb*

> *Birds sing on a bare bough*
> *O believer, canst not thou?*
>
> *Charles Haddon Spurgeon,* Salt Cellars

"Now onto the next component of faith: *belief.* After we want something, we've got to believe that we will acquire that desire; we've got to believe that the desire will come true."

"Does that mean that I should be able to picture myself having the desire?"

"Absolutely. You should be able to picture that desire as if it already happened. Even though that desire has not physically appeared, you should still be able to experience a warm, assuring feeling inside, knowing that the manifestation of the desire is to come."

## Trust

*In God I have put my trust; I will not be afraid what man can do unto me.*

Psalms LVI, 11 c. 1500 BC

"The next component of faith is *trust*. You've utilized this component before, Wonder?"

"Of course, I've trusted people with secrets or with my stuff or with money."

"That same trust can be applied with desires. Before we discuss the last three components of faith, I want to digress a minute to the concepts of 'Second Force' or 'Desire Testers.'"

His eyebrows raised and danced twice. "You mean that in addition to having God place challenges before our desires, there are also other challenges placed before our desires?"

"You've got it, Wonder! You remember the laws of physics from school? For every action, there is an equal and opposing reaction. Thus, when we set a goal or have a desire, an opposing force challenges that goal or desire. This is also known as Second Force. The First Force is our desire or goal. Soon after that goal or desire exists, challenges will start to occur. To surmount Second Force, the latter three components of faith — trust, surrender, and knowing — are absolutely essential."

"So are you saying that even though it may look like my desire will not be achieved, that is just Second Force? I must trust that Second Force will leave and my desire will happen?"

"Yes. Although Second Force may appear to be long lasting, it does eventually get replaced by your desire."

Wonder chewed absentmindedly on his pen cap and squinted his left eye forming a question. "So, how does trust differ from belief?"

"Belief focuses more upon picturing the desire — being able to feel that the desire can happen. Trust is more of a focus of attention. Initially, attention is on the desire; then Second Force comes along and commands attention. Trust is the process or instrument used to redirect the attention from Second Force back to desire."

"Okay, it's sort of making sense. Are there other components?"

## SURRENDER

*There is a time to let things happen and a time to make things happen.*

*Hugh Prather*

"Yes. Next is *surrender*. Wonder, what do you know about surrender?"

"I guess I have some unpleasant images of surrender. We surrender when we're on the losing side of a war, or in an argument, which in essence means giving up control and being controlled by others," he answered in a voice that faintly suggested anger and fear.

"Right. Using surrender as a component of faith might seem absurd. Just when Second Force comes in to challenge our desire, we are being asked to surrender or release any control that we might direct toward protecting that desire; we are asked *not* to try to make that desire happen."

"That does sound kinda nuts. But when my sister had her baby, she was told to relax, to surrender instead of fighting the powerful contractions."

"Exactly. The surrender process is twofold. First, it is a surrendering of will or a surrendering of control to God. You've no doubt heard the expression, 'Let go and let God.'"

"Yes," Wonder assured her, "I know that expression in my sleep."

"Second it is a letting go of resistance. Margaret Pounders tells us, 'The tighter we pull, the harder the knot becomes. We have to ease up, allow the thread of circumstances to relax, then take whatever action to remove the tangled situation from our life.' She goes on to say, 'When we resent a person, that person clings to us. When we resent a condition, that condition draws its life from the strength of our negative attitude.' And as we all know, Wonder, that which we resist, persists."

"So how does this relate to all the other components and then to faith?"

"First, you have a desire to be something, to do something, or to have something. You believe that your desire is possible by picturing or experiencing it. Then Second Force comes to challenge your desire. Despite outer conditions, you trust that your desire will still occur. You spend time redirecting your belief from Second Force back to your desire. Second Force is quite powerful. You are inclined to want to control situations and events to make your desire happen. Instead, you do the opposite by doing nothing (surrender) to control the people or events that challenge your desire; you let God be the pilot."

"I'm following you. What comes next?"

## KNOWING

"The next component of faith that is essential in conquering Second Force is *knowing*."

"I'm just thinking back to the other components. I guess that knowing is stronger than believing and stronger than trusting?"

"You've got it! Remember that believing focuses upon giving substance to the possibility of your desires happening. Knowing occurs after all of the other components have been utilized — rather like the 'icing on the cake' idea. After the desire and the control of the desire have been turned over to God, you just sit back and know that the desire will occur."

Wonder interrupted. "Let me make sure I understand. This sitting back is not laziness, right? It's more of a resting or waiting? In my own situation of working to be a marketing rep, there comes a time when I know it will happen when I stop *making* situations and people do what I want."

"Yes. Also, remember that *knowing* involves complete concentration and focus upon the desire rather than on what is happening in the outer. Let me share an image with you. Picture a woman walking confidently on a tightrope. She concentrates fully upon her desire to walk across the tightrope. She does not allow any of her mental energy to nourish the worry of slipping off the tightrope. She does not play the sabotage game. She does not think: 'What if I fall? What if the rope breaks?' She remains focused for she *knows* that she will successfully walk across the tightrope."

"I understand. Is Second Force still present in this stage of faith?"

"Yes. Second Force is present. However, knowing is also quite strong for it insists that the desire will be achieved without your doing anything about it."

WALKING THE TALK

Wonder looked out the window for a moment. How could he possibly get from desire to knowing in the workplace? It seemed impossible. He turned and studied Wisdom for a moment. Well, it couldn't be impossible, after all Wisdom had done it! And probably many times.

During Wonder's reflection, Wisdom had taken the opportunity to pour some water. She offered him some.

"Any questions?" she asked.

"Of course. Now for my favorite part! How I can put your wise words into practice?"

"Well, let's begin by discovering your desire for something. In the Bible it is written, 'Where there is no vision, the people perish' (Prov.

29:18). You must have a vision or desire in order to lead a fulfilling life. The desires exist; it's just a matter of discovering them."

"Okay, I buy into the concept, but how do I do that?"

"Identify what some of the things are that you enjoy doing. Identify your values in life. Identify your strengths and weaknesses. Also, spend some time in your inner silence asking what is your heart's desire. See if you can identify any of your desires with the words of Emmet Fox that you shared earlier. This should lead you to something that you'd like to do or be in the workplace."

Wisdom rose from her chair.

"As a matter of fact, I need to check something in the PR department; so why don't you think about that for a little bit, and I'll be right back," she said as moved toward the door.

When she returned, Wonder was ready.

"Okay. I've now identified several desires. I've also identified a heart's desire. It is something I have known, but until your explanation, I did not realize the magnitude of this desire."

Wisdom looked at him attentively. He took a deep breath.

"I'm ready to be a marketing rep."

"Now you must believe that your desires will come true. Thomas Troward tells us, 'Having seen and felt the end, you have willed the means to the realization of the end.' Therefore, Wonder, can you picture what it would be like to achieve your heart's desire?"

"Oh, yes! I can imagine myself in that role. I see myself doing marketing responsibilities. I see myself utilizing the positive techniques I've researched for years. I also see the outstanding interaction and contentment in those people I deal with. I feel my own happiness while at work and when I reflect upon what I've completed each day for my manager."

Wisdom provided a strong nod of approval. "You have a very good image going, Wonder. Work with that image daily to strengthen your belief. I'll share with you a few other techniques that can be used to strengthen your belief. The first is credited to Catherine Ponder who discusses it in her book, *Open Your Mind to Prosperity*. That technique focuses upon creating a Wheel of Fortune."

"Not a wheel for my car, right?"

"Mmmm. No. A Wheel of Fortune is typically made out of a large sheet of poster board that is cut in the shape of a circle. Poster board can even be selected according to a particular color, for the ancients believed that colors carry particular types of energy. For example, gold or green is used for prosperity. Red or pink is used for love. Orange or yellow is used for health. Blue is used for intellectual achievement while white is used for spiritual matters. In your case, for your career desire, you may choose your favorite color or one of the ancient colors," Wisdom explained.

"Okay, so now I've chosen a color. What do I do next?"

"You might paste your picture on the circle. You can also have the title Marketing Rep pasted there. On your existing business card, you can white out your existing title and print Marketing Rep. You can then paste this on your circle. You can paste dollar amounts you'd like to earn or names of clients that you'd like to have. You might also like to add some typed-up affirmations to your wheel such as 'I am a very successful Marketing Rep' or 'I perform my work easily through the power of my Higher Self.' An excellent affirmation is 'I am grateful for this or something better for the highest and best of all concerned. Amen.' In this manner, you are allowing the very best to happen."

"I can handle that. What would I then do with the Wheel? Surely I couldn't bring it to work," he asked blushing at even the thought.

"Very astute!" Wisdom said laughing. "Instead, place it in your home where you can see it several times in the day. Perhaps in your bedroom so you can view it when you awaken and when you go to sleep — when your subconscious is receptive to images and words since your mind is in the alpha state at those times."

"Sounds good!" Wonder was filling with confidence. These techniques and activities might actually work and make his trip on the fast track easier and speedier.

"Another technique that you can use to strengthen your belief is to create an Image Book. Buy a three-ring binder, a spiral notebook, or a magnetic photo album. Select images and affirmations as in the Wheel of Fortune. Arrange them in the album or notebook. Some people even like to combine the use of a Wheel of Fortune and an Image Book."

"Cool idea. Any others?"

"Yes. Some people create success posters. Catherine Ponder writes about a successful businessman who was often asked, 'How's business?' His reply always was, 'Business is wonderful because there's gold dust in the air!' You can borrow his saying and make a poster with 'Business is wonderful because there's gold dust in the air' on it; then add some glue and sprinkle gold glitter on it. Then you'll always remember that there is prosperity and gold dust all around you. If you get discouraged because a client refuses your sales, glance at the gold dust poster. One of the quickest ways to fail in sales is to have negative or limiting thoughts. A gold dust poster reminds you to keep focused on success. It's not magic that makes things happen; it's focus and affirmations that work!"

"I could get into this. I used to love art class in school. And my sister has a bunch of art supplies to keep her kids occupied. I'm sure she'll let me borrow some."

"Especially if you include the kids! You can create any variety of posters — and even include scripture verses on them if you like."

"Sounds great. My apartment could use some decorating!"

"Don't forget about written or verbal affirmations. An example of an affirmation might be, 'On or before _____ date, I will be a marketing rep.' The key is repetition — write or say your belief many times a day, even a hundred times a day."

"I enjoy writing affirmations, so that one will be easy."

"Good. Now, let's move on to our third component, trust. This involves redirecting or refocusing attention. Initially, attention may be on a particular goal but it may get redirected toward a fear or a worry. When your attention wanders, refocus on your goal. Spend time visualizing your goal to strengthen your belief. When fear or worry occurs, counter with a pair of denials and affirmations. If your goal, Wonder, is to be a marketing rep and if you were suddenly transferred to another position such as a clerical position, you might silently state, 'This is not my truth. My truth is to be a marketing rep.'"

"Okay. So what about surrender? That's the hard one."

"Surrender focuses on the letting go process. This phase will probably happen to you when you are close to achieving your heart's desire of being a marketing rep. However, challenges may occur that may make you believe that you are losing your heart's desire. For example, maybe you had been doing proposals and are now suddenly switched to doing pure clerical work. Instead of trying to control events and people, it is important to let go, to let events and people pass."

"That's great advice, but how?"

"The key to letting go is nonresistance. In order to receive your heart's desire quickly, you must let go of any resentment toward the obstacles that are appearing to hold you back. That means letting go of any hurt, bitterness, or negative thoughts about your situation. You can supplement nonresistance with denials and affirmations."

Nodding, Wonder affirmed, "I can handle that."

"Great. There's a little more about surrender you need to know. After you've released any energy that has bound you to another person, you must also release your will to God's will. Again, a repetition of affirmations gives you strength. My personal favorites are:

"Not my will but thy will.

> "Dear ego, dear thoughts, it's okay for you
> to take some quiet time. Relax and be still. I now
> invite God's will to facilitate the outcome of this
> situation. I relax and feel the will of God as a
> peaceful power that moves from my head to my
> feet and to my world. I affirm that all is good."

Wonder realized that he was learning this stuff quickly, and he attributed it to his teacher's skill and the fact that she practiced these lessons herself. *She really "walks her talk,"* he thought. He glanced at his watch. Their hour was almost over.

"And now we get to knowing. What are some affirmations I can use to help with knowing?" he asked.

Wisdom replied with some suggestions:

> "I have absolute confidence that I am guided
> to my true place of employment.

> "I know that there is absolute Love and Har-
> mony in all of my business interactions.

> "I know exactly what to do in all situations."

"Well, you've given me a lot to think about — as usual!" he said as he stood and prepared to go back to his office.

"One more thing Wonder. Another helpful aid for knowing is to spend time, in quiet, visualizing your good — for in the silence there is strength. The silence and imagery will increase your ability to know."

"That makes sense. So now I have to practice all this stuff. Can we meet in a week?"

"Sounds great to me. How about Thursday at 10?"

"Great. See you then!"

When Wonder arrived at his office, the unit's secretary handed him an envelope marked "Urgent." He entered his office, sat down, and tore into it, anticipating a new, exciting project.

New was a correct assessment, but it was far from exciting. Wonder felt sick as he reread the words. His "special project" was to perform start-up administrative duties for his co-worker who had just been awarded the marketing rep position that Wonder had also applied for.

Wonder attempted to breathe through the pain. It helped a little, but tears still welled up in his eyes. It was 11:30; he decided to skip lunch and go for a walk in a nearby park. Perhaps the fresh air would clear his head.

BIBLIOGRAPHY

Fox,.Emmet. *Power Through Constructive Thinking.* New York: Harper & Row, 1940.

Pounders, Margaret. *Laws of Love.* Unity Village, Mo.: Unity Village, 1979.

*You give but little when you give of your possessions. It is when you give of yourself that you truly give . . . There are those who give little of the much they have — and they give for recognition and their hidden desire makes their gifts unwholesome . . . And there are those who give with pain, and that pain is their baptism. And there are those who give and know not pain in giving, nor do they seek joy, nor give with mindfulness of virtue; they give as in yonder valley the myrtle breathes its fragrance into space. Through the hands of these God speaks, and from behind their eyes He smiles upon the earth.*

*Kahlil Gibran,* The Prophet

*Giving means extending one's Love with no conditions, no expectations, and no boundaries... having no desire to get anything from, or to change another person.*

*Gerald Jampolsky, M.D.,*
Love Is Letting Go of Fear

*The highest reward for man's toil is not what he gets for it, but what he becomes by it.*

*John Ruskin*

*seven*

# GIVING

Wisdom's office was beginning to feel like home to Wonder. He looked forward to sinking down in the comfortable chair, sharing with her his week's spiritual adventures and listening to her guidance and lessons. But this day he entered her office looking like her once abandoned Himalayan cat: dejected and just a tad scruffy — something Wisdom had not seen in him before.

"Hi," was all he could muster.

"Hi, yourself," answered Wisdom with a sympathetic and inviting tone.

Silence. Wonder stared out the window.

"I guess we know each other well enough for me to ask you what's wrong?" Wisdom probed.

"You can tell?"

Wisdom laughed. "It's pretty obvious."

"Yeah, I guess it is."

"Want to talk about it?"

"Yeah." More silence.

Then Wonder straightened up a little and began to tell Wisdom about his new assignment. When he had finished, he slumped back in the chair and said, "So you see after all the work we've been doing, this is a real setback."

"This is terrific!" Wisdom exclaimed and Wonder looked at her incredulously.

"Terrific? Why do you say that? I think it's awful!"

"This week's lesson is about giving. And you have just been asked to assist someone who you feel has taken a job that is rightfully yours. What better way to discover how to truly give than in this circumstance," Wisdom explained.

"If you insist. But you are going to have to show me how I can eke out even a shred of optimism from this situation," Wonder commented in a slightly less dejected tone.

"Oh, I intend to," Wisdom promised. She grew quiet for a moment and gazed out her window as if trying to make up her mind about something.

"Change is an interesting situation, Wonder. We long for it and yet when it presents itself, sometimes we feel confused and anxious."

"You sound like you have something on your mind? Contemplating some changes?" Wonder intuitively asked.

"Perhaps, perhaps," Wisdom said, and then turned back toward her student. "But for now let's get on with our lessons! Have you been doing the reading I suggested, the works by Kahlil Gibran?"

"Yes, I have and I have a lot of questions. What did Gibran mean when he wrote: 'There are those who give with pain and that is their baptism?' Isn't giving supposed to be a joyous process?"

"As you can see from your present circumstance, giving is not always joyous in the business world. Can you think of some other situations where giving is not joyous?"

"Well, let's see . . . How about . . .

> "When an actor is asked to do her boss's work because her boss doesn't know how to do it, then the actor may resist sharing her talent so her boss can shine;

"When an actor works lots of overtime and is not appreciated, then she may not want to give more of her time since no one appears to care;

"When an actor is asked to train someone he knows will be taking his job, then he may not want to share his knowledge;

"When an actor knows that the sooner he finishes his outstanding tasks, the sooner his job will be down-sized, then he may not want to give his skills in a timely manner;

"Or when an actor receives a demotion due to a false accusation, then he may not want to give freely to his successor."

"Very good, Wonder. Do you understand now how giving is sometimes a painful situation?"

"That depends. In the examples I mentioned, do you *honestly* expect actors to willingly give?"

"Yes, I *honestly* do."

"That's impossible! I think those actors should be able to walk away and say, 'No way. I don't have to take this.' It's just too painful to give under those circumstances."

## BAPTISM

"I agree, Wonder, these career actors are certainly free to walk away. And that may be the best solution if there is greater good out there for them at another place of employment. However, if there is not another job available immediately, then few people have the luxury to walk away; thus, learning to give willingly is an important asset for business survival. And, yes, giving in these situations may be painful.

That is, of course, why Gibran says that, 'There are those who give with pain and that pain is their baptism.'"

"Okay. I understand the pain of giving, but what about the baptism?"

"There are two parts of baptism. In the *Metaphysical Bible Dictionary*, Charles Fillmore tells us that the first baptism represents cleansing, dissolving, purging, dropping the old, and letting go. In the business world, our giving through the pain is analogous to John's Baptism. There is a cleansing, a dissolving, or a dropping of the ego, the pride, and the personal will."

Wonder grimaced. "That doesn't sound appealing to me. I think I'd rather only give partially as long as I didn't lose my job. What good could possibly be gained in giving with pain?"

"Well, there's always part two of the baptism process. According to Fillmore, the second baptism represents affirmation, regeneration, and taking hold, for it is a spiritual baptism. After we've gone through the process of giving with pain, we're ready to use that pain as our springboard into greatness; we're ready to create a pearl from that irritation."

"What's the greatness? A better job? More money? What do you mean by pearl?"

"That pearl which we acquire from giving with pain is 'unconditional giving.' That is, we are able to give to anyone and under any circumstance freely. When we are able to give unconditionally, we experience joy and peace of mind during the whole time that we are giving. Our giving process is then a very rewarding time!"

"It sure sounds great!"

"It is more than great. Here's what Gibran shares with us: 'Through the hands of these God speaks, and from behind their eyes He smiles upon the earth.' You see, Wonder, when you are giving and you have earned the 'unconditional giving' experience of God smiling through you, your body feels a laughter that licks your insides; your eyes feel delight that dews them; and your soul skips and shimmers from His smile!"

"I don't know what to say except that it sounds like an intense moment of giving. Once this two-phase baptism has occurred, what sorts of gifts do we receive?"

## THE GIFTS

"One of the benefits for actors when they are giving is that they automatically create a channel for love. Quite often, business people wish they could love others, but emotions like hurt, envy, and bitterness stand in the way. Giving opens this channel of 'love' so that it easily passes between two people."

"So you're saying that if I've been challenged by a business person who is difficult to love, that I should try to give something to her? This will help me to love?"

"Exactly. It's like magic — spiritual magic, that is."

"Okay. I'll *give* it a try!"

"Another benefit of giving is that it opens up opportunities for us. It primes our pump!"

"What *are* you talking about?"

"Perhaps pumps were a little bit before your time, Wonder. 'Priming the pump' is an old metaphor. In today's time, this concept might be better explained in this story by Jose Silva:

"'A man walking through the desert was desperate for a drink of water. He was certain that he was dying of thirst. Suddenly in the distance he saw an old pump standing by a lone cactus.

"'He got closer and saw a flask of water there too. On the flask of water was a sign that read, 'Danger! Warning!' When he reached the pump, he found that there was a piece of paper attached to the warning sign. He unfolded the paper and read the following on it:

> "'Thirsty traveler, you must have faith. There is enough water in this little flask to quench your thirst for the moment, but the next oasis is more than 100 miles distant. You will never make it on this one drink of water; you will surely die if you try. But if you pour this water down the pump, the water will prime the pump, wet the leather washer, and the pump will then provide all the cool, clear water you need.'

"So you see, Wonder, it is important for you to first give in the business world if you want to receive."

"Give what?"

"Give many things. Elbert Hubbard tells us, 'People who never do any more than they're paid to do are never paid any more than they do.' Thus, it is often necessary for employees to walk extra miles in order to receive a higher salary, recognition, or a position. It is often necessary for marketing reps to give whatever is applicable to their clients if they want to receive the opportunity to provide their clients with services or goods. It is often necessary for managers to give whatever is applicable if they want to have-long term working relationships with their employees."

"So, you probably expect me to take this new position with a smile? To give to the new marketing rep and then it will be my turn?"

"Well, not exactly. The secret is that you must *never* stop giving, Wonder."

## THE WAITING AND THE RESTORATION

Wonder looked out the window for awhile and sipped at the tea Wisdom had brought him earlier. He found that he was drinking more tea — herbal tea — and that somehow he felt calmer since he had cut down on his caffeine consumption. He wanted to ask a question, but he hesitated.

"Please understand that I don't intend to be disrespectful with this question. Sometimes, we give and give, yet we don't receive. In essence, we've primed the pump, yet we remain waiting for that water to come out, or in some instances, that water does come out but is stolen by someone who has not even been priming."

"That's really two questions, and I don't interpret them as being disrespectful. Let me first address your issues concerning the long or seemingly endless wait. Margaret Pounders tells us, 'When God wants an oak, He spends a hundred years. But he can make a squash in only two months . . . A squash is good for only one meal, but an oak provides shade and beauty for generations.'

"Perhaps, someone's good or success is so lofty that it takes time for it to grow to fruition. This is often the case with career goals — especially one that is a heart's desire. Keep in mind that for the person who has endured challenges that seem endless and has finally attained his business goal, success will be limitless! 'Desires are nourished by delays,' if I may quote John Ray from his *English Proverbs*," Wisdom explained.

"That's certainly encouraging for business goals. However, what about those of us who walk extra miles for a manager who doesn't appreciate us?" Wonder asked.

"Giving is still important so don't stop walking those extra miles. Ralph Waldo Emerson tells us, 'If you serve an ungrateful master, serve him the more. Put God in your debt. Every stroke shall be repaid. The longer the payment is witholden, the better for you; for compound interest on compound interest is the rate and usage of this exchequer.'"

"So every mile I walk I can liken to money I deposit in the bank? My miles, like my money, earn interest. When the divinely directed withdrawal finally occurs, I'll have a prosperous, successful workplace investment?"

"You're right on target, Wonder! There's a point I forgot to mention. Whenever you give or walk extra miles, you may not always receive from the person or company in which you gave."

"How so?"

"Some actors walk miles upon miles for their organization and receive no reward. Yet, they may later be rewarded by attaining great success from another job offer or from a profitable hobby. Rewards are often recognized in other ways or at other times. You know how sometimes you help someone, and then someone different ends up coming to your rescue?"

"Okay, I understand that sometimes we must wait for our rewards, which may or may not come back to us from the recipient of our gifts. But now, getting back to my second question, what about when we actually see our good being taken by someone else?"

"Remember when God spoke to Joel and said: 'I will restore to you the years which the swarming locust has eaten' (Joel 2:25). The eaten years are analogous to opportunities you may have felt were stolen from you, most painfully represented in your current dilemma."

"That's for sure! It seems like opportunities or rewards go to the locusts who are good game players or 'bottom kissers' as we like to say."

"Wonder, it is true that those opportunities or rewards may have been eaten by workplace locusts. But don't focus on that. Think instead of the greater good that may come to you in the future."

"It's hard to believe in this restoration process. Can you share with me some affirmations?"

"Gladly. Consider the following:

"I quickly and eagerly attract my highest good to me. I am receptive to Divine Timing and I wait patiently in peace.

"There is no such thing as loss for Divine Restoration gives me an even better (job, promotion, office, project . . .) than I ever imagined. I attract my perfect (job, promotion, office, project) with confidence and power.

"I love you (parties involved). I bless you and I behold the Divine in you. I remove any negative thoughts that I've attached to you. I now fill my life with God's Restoration that brings me overflowing fulfillment and enjoyment."

"Thanks," Wonder said, scribbling down some notes so he could remember these tools. "They'll help. Now for my favorite part. How can I manifest these actions? What gifts can I give?"

## WALKING THE TALK

"It's really a personal matter what you give, and over time and with experience, you will begin to sense the right gifts. But I will give you a few examples among gifts I have given over the years.

"Rebates for various purchased items are a neat business gift. When completing a rebate form, you simply list an associate's name rather than your own name. This is a handy gift if it's awkward for you to actually give something to a particular workplace person. With rebates, you as the giver can remain anonymous!

"Magazines can be given to other business people or be left in a cafeteria or lobby.

"If you are a manager you can regularly give your employees TOAs (Tokens of Appreciation) which can include humorous articles, baked goods, Thank You notes, time, birthday cards, handshakes, smiles . . . the list is as endless as your imagination.

"If you are a marketing rep, you can also give many of the above TOAs. For all morning marketing calls, be sure to bring along some form of baked goods.

"Welcoming Letters are a wonderful gift that managers can give to new employees as they come on board.

"Thank You notes to clients, associates, bosses, and employees are always a perfect form of appreciation."

IDEAS FOR NONMATERIAL GIFTS

"How about nonmaterial gifts? How can I share in that way?

"Of course, Wonder. Here are a few notes on ideas I have had." Wisdom presented Wonder with yet another neatly typed handout for his ever-growing notebook.

"Christin Rossetti gave me an idea through her poem 'What can

I give Him poor as I am? / If I were a shepherd I would bring a lamb. / If I were a wise man I would do my part. / Yet, what can I give Him, give my heart.' So in our own situations, we can give our heart or our love in a platonic manner to another corporate actor."

"What else?" Wonder asked.

"We can share love, light, or blessings silently with others. We can do this by slightly extending our hand toward the particular person, office, car, or building and thinking or silently saying 'love,' 'light,' or 'blessings.' We can imagine any of those qualities being shared from us to another person."

"How about this one: In the winter, we might enjoy scraping off the snow from a particular actor's car windows," Wonder jumped in.

Wisdom continued with her ideas.

"You might think about creating an 'Appreciation List.' On a regular basis (daily, weekly, or monthly), list all of the things that you appreciate. This is especially important in areas in which you feel most challenged. For example, if you feel challenged by your manager, then make a list of all those qualities that you appreciate about him. Perhaps initially, it may only be a particular shirt or tie he wears. In time, your list will expand. If you feel challenged by a boring job, then let your appreciation list focus upon its good aspects. Perhaps you may appreciate dealing with people or being able to make a difference.

"Last, if you feel challenged by your environment, then let your Appreciation List focus upon that. You might appreciate the comfortable chair that you're sitting on, your office furniture, having a safe working environment, or having cleaning services provided."

"Thank you, Wisdom, for such creative gifts. I'm sure they'll be very important study aids for all of us actors."

"No problem. Over time, you'll start thinking up your own. Now especially is a good time for you to put some of these into practice. You have a rare opportunity to give consciously in a situation that I know is very painful for you. Yet, I know you can do it."

"You are right. This is a big challenge. But thanks to your help, maybe I'll make it through. I guess it was no accident that I came and spoke with you when I did."

Mindful of time, and eager to get back to his new duties with passion instead of resentment, Wonder added, "So when shall we meet next?"

"Well, Wonder, I'm having some co-workers and friends over for a Tofu BBQ next weekend. I'd like you to join us; perhaps we will get a chance to talk about the hallowedness of laughter and how it fits in the workplace environment."

"Sure. I wouldn't miss this! I'll need directions?"

"Of course. I'll email you the directions and time. See you then."

"Thanks," Wonder said as he left. He bounced down the hall with a feeling of excitement. He was honored to be included in Wisdom's life outside the workplace.

## BIBLIOGRAPHY

Emerson, Ralph Waldo. "Compensation." In *The Harvard Classics*. Vol. 5. Edited by Charles W. Eliot. New York: P.F. Collier & Son, 1909.

Emerson, Ralph Waldo. "Essays on English Traits." In *The Harvard Classics*. Vol. 5. Edited by Charles W. Eliot. New York: P.F. Collier & Son, 1909.

Gibran, Kahlil. *The Prophet*. New York: Alfred A. Knopf, 1979.

Pounders, Margaret. *Laws of Love*. Unity Village, Mo.: Unity Books, 1979.

Silva, Jose and Ed Bernd, Jr. *Sales Power: The Silva Mind Method for Sales Professionals*. New York: Putnam Publishing Group, 1992.

*Laughter is a tranquilizer with no side effects.*
*Arnold H. Glasow*

*The person who knows how to laugh at himself will never cease to be amused.*
*Shirley MacLaine*

*Against the assault of laughter, nothing can stand.*
*Mark Twain*

*A person without a sense of humor is like a wagon without springs—jolted by every possible pebble on the road.*
*Henry Ward Beecher*

*A well-developed sense of humor is the pole that adds balance to your steps as you walk the tightrope of life.*
*William A. Ward*

*The most acutely suffering animal on earth invented laughter.*
*Friedrich Nietzsche*

*eight*

# HALLOWED BE THY HUMOR

Wonder glanced at the wrinkled, ripped paper that contained his emailed directions to Wisdom's home. Traffic and a few morning errands had put him behind, and by the time he came to her street, he was already an hour late for the party.

*Geeze, I didn't know there were houses back here. Pretty nice area — still part of town yet a bit away from it*, Wonder noticed. He parked behind a long line of cars, imagining that everyone in the city was at Wisdom's party. As he walked toward the house, he did a double take when he noticed the company president's car.

*One never knows*, he smiled to himself.

On his right, he noticed a flower garden resembling an island. White birch, Japanese palms, flowers of pink, purple, yellow, and white inhabited the island with the waterfall. What he would give to have regular access to that natural, soothing sound! And of course, there were the two white wrought iron benches. Wonder imagined Wisdom sitting there with a special person. *A perfect place for meditation and revitalization — and learning*, he mused. He noticed two squirrels chasing up and down a tree. Quite near, another squirrel acrobatically hung upside down to sneak a few sunflower seeds from the bird feeder.

*Cool place*, he mused as he moved up the steps. Approaching the landing he smiled at the marble angels adorning the top of the railing.

*What'd you think she'd have — lions or something?* he chattered in his mind. *Hmmm. Should I use the brass door knob or door bell. I never know. Ahh, what the heck, I'll ring.* From inside he heard the sound of children.

"I'll get it mom."

"No. I want to get it. No fair! You had a head start. Mommm. Tell him to let me get the door."

The door opened and the giggling, tugging boys greeted Wonder's surprised gaze.

Wisdom was soon at the top of the steps and her loose, long hair flagged like a drying pillowcase on a breezy line.

"Guys, upstairs please. Wonder, I see you met my sons. I am so glad you could make it. Please come in."

In a matter of seconds, Wonder felt a force brush his legs as another child pushed his way eagerly into the abode.

"Aren't you ready to come to my sleep-over yet? Come on. Let's gooo," beckoned the neighbor's son to Wisdom's sons.

Her sons soon lifted their packed sports sacks that rested in the corner and exchanged their good-byes and kisses with mom.

They departed amid a cacophony of loud noise as the three boys practiced putting their mouths on their arms, blowing air in a way that mimicked passing gas. For the grand finale, as they bounced down the front walk, they put their hands under their arm pits and flapped to create yet another interesting sound.

"The abandon of the young," Wonder said, recalling his own childhood.

Wisdom rolled her eyes and sighed.

"Please come in and excuse my amateur comedians. Since they found out they're allowed to attend the neighbor's sleep-over, they've been a bit wound up."

"No problem, Wisdom. Nice house."

"Thanks. Let me point out the logistics. Bathrooms are there and there. Food is in there. Beverages and nonalcoholic cocktails are over there. Most of the guests are already outside, so feel free to explore and mingle. I may not always be around, so just introduce yourself. You'll know some people from the office, and others are my personal friends."

"Well if the welcoming committee is any indication, I guess everyone is having a good time!"

"Hopefully with a little more tasteful humor — but you never know. Are you aware, Wonder, that humor is a marvelous spiritual tool?"

"Get going! I thought spirituality was supposed to be serious and solemn."

Wonder felt a lesson coming on, and admired Wisdom's calm. Here she was the hostess of a party, and she was taking time to offer him yet another lesson.

"Oh no, dear Wonder. Even in Psalms 2:4, it is written, 'He that dwells in heaven shall laugh.' Remember that dwelling in heaven refers to being in that inner, peaceful, Divine filled space throughout our human existence."

"So, laughter is very closely linked with our spirituality — to the experiencing of the inner kingdom of heaven?" Wonder questioned.

"Absolutely. Jesus tells us, 'Truly I say to you, He who will not receive the kingdom of God like a little child will never enter into it' (Luke 18:17). One of the ways children receive the kingdom of God is through laughter. Just out of curiosity, Wonder, how many times a day do you think a child and adult laugh?"

"Oh, I would guess that a child laughs about fifty times a day and an adult about twenty-five times a day."

"Well, I have heard that the average child laughs about five hundred times a day and the average adult laughs about fifteen times a day."

"Amazing! I guess can learn something from children about humor. Maybe I should follow your kids to the sleep-over!"

Wisdom smiled at Wonder's lightheartedness.

"And did you know that many of the highly developed souls have physical counterparts who regularly laugh, smile, or share humor with others. Laughter and a sense of humor are the diamonds/pearls/peonies in our life, born from challenges that often mean pain and tears. 'Blessed are you who weep now, for you shall laugh' (Luke 6:21).

"Come with me, Wonder. I'll talk while I show you to the garden and introduce you to some other guests."

HALLOWING THE PHYSICAL

> *"I will smile and my digestion will improve; I will chuckle and my burdens will be lightened; I will laugh and my life will be lengthened for this is the great secret of long life and now it is mine. I will laugh at the world."*
> Og Mandino, The Greatest Salesman in the World

"So how does laughter benefit the physical part of us?" Wonder asked as they walked through the house.

"I'm not going to tell you," Wisdom gleamed girlishly.

"What do you mean? Are you leaving me in suspense?"

"Of course not. *I'm* not going to tell you. I will let a *friend of mine* tell you."

"All right. Carry on then."

"Great. Let's go."

Wisdom turned a brass doorknob and opened a pair of white French doors leading to the backyard. Wonder gasped at the beauty that called, "Look at me first, look at me first," from every direction. Mature weeping willows gracefully guarded the edges of the property. The backyard boasted clusters of oaks, some of which were connected with hammocks. Scattered elsewhere were bird baths and feeders, a frog sand box, a wooden swing set, two small rose gardens, a vegetable garden, and a pool that looked as if it came from the pages of *Architectural Digest*. Wonder was impressed with its beauty, serenity, and diversity. On this special day, Wisdom had accentuated the already picturesque backyard with gold and white decorations, the same as in the house. It seemed to bring a peace and harmony to the jubilant goings on.

Wonder's attention was next grabbed by the sounds of laughter and conversation spilling over along with splashes of water from the pool. As he noticed familiar faces of workers, he thought how odd it was to see company folks in bathing suits, pig noses, Groucho glasses, Hawaiian lei, flippers, and other odd combos of jocularity. Co-workers, normally dignified and focused, now ran from the wet grass jumping, diving, and scrambling for inner tubes that bobbed on the turbulent water.

"Wheeee. That water's cold!" Wisdom exclaimed as a large splash soaked her legs. People formed the letters of YMCA as the song blared from the speakers. The personnel director passed around Sombrero Hats in anticipation of the next song: the Mexican Hat dance.

"Seems like you really have some party animals here," Wonder said as Wisdom sat down near him.

"You betcha!"

Wonder watched the final contestant for the Limbo do his feat.

"George, congratulations," hollered Wisdom.

"Oh hi, Wisdom! Thanks. You know how I love to do the Limbo."

"George, I'd like you to meet an associate, Wonder. And Wonder, I'd like you to meet George who works as a principal of a local school."

They exchanged handshakes and greetings. Suddenly they were both enveloped in a stream of water that seemed to come from nowhere.

"I'll get you, Maggie!" George yelled as he shook his arms and wagged his tongue. Wonder caught sight of a women, Maggie, running away holding a water pistol high in the air.

"In your dreams, George, in your dreams," giggled Maggie.

"Sorry, Wisdom. My attention is now yours."

"George, you know how I've admired the way you use physical humor to help you with workplace challenges. Are you open to sharing with my guest?'

"Certainly, my dear Wisdom, certainly. Wonder was your name, right?"

"Yes, sir."

"Just because I'm a principal, don't stand on ceremony. Skip the sir and call me George."

"Okay, George," Wonder grinned.

"Let's sit down. Away from where we might get soaked again!"

"Sure. How about over there," Wonder said, pointing to three chairs beneath a shade tree. "So, you're a principal?"

"Yes. At a large urban school. It's rough compared to schools thirty years ago. Now we do more than educate. We have to deal with drugs, alcohol, and guns. Despite all these side attractions, I still have teachers who want to teach and students who want to learn," he said.

"How do you handle it?"

"Initially, not very well. I developed physical symptoms such as ulcers, muscle spasms, shortness of breath, hives, migraines, and one cold after another. I could barely function some days. In my search for a solution, I discovered humor. I noticed that when I laughed I felt better, so I decided to make humor a regular part of my life. And from that point on, my physical discomforts left."

"Please don't take this as an insult, but how do you know that you really got a physical cure and that it wasn't just in your head. Is there any sort of medical proof?"

"Wisdom, I like your friend's inquisitiveness," laughed George. "Wonder, if it's facts you want, I'll quote some medical experts. Dr.

Walsh, a medical director for the School of Sociology at Fordham University, found that hearty laughter stimulates our internal organs and increases our immunity against disease 'Laughter has the effect of brushing aside many of the worries and fears that set a stage for sickness,' he is quoted as saying in a book by Norman Cousins called *Head First: The Biology of Hope.*"

"So the more we laugh, the more we increase our immunity to disease?" asked Wonder.

"Precisely," interjected Wisdom. "George, if you don't mind, I'd like to share what I recall from my reading on that subject."

"Be my guest, Wisdom," George said, making a little gesture reminiscent of Charlie Chaplin.

"Thank you, my dear," Wisdom bowed. "Dr. William Fry, Jr., of the Department of Psychiatry at Stanford Medical School, compares laughter to exercise. Cousins mentioned him as well. Laughter 'causes huffing and puffing, speeds up the heart rate, raises blood pressure, accelerates breathing, increases oxygen consumption, gives the muscles of the face and stomach a workout, and relaxes muscles not involved in laughing. Twenty seconds of laughter, he has contended, can double the heart rate for three to five minutes. This is the equivalent of three minutes of strenuous rowing,' Cousins wrote."

"So we should add laughter as a regular routine with our other exercises," Wonder reasoned.

"Absolutely," commented Wisdom. "Ideally, a routine of physical, spiritual, and humor exercises would help us be stronger to deal with our corporate teachers and tests."

George added some other advice.

"Laughter stimulates our brains to produce *catecholamine,* which prepares us for fight or flight. This, in turn, stimulates the release of endorphins. In fact, Norman Cousins found that ten hours of belly laughter produced two hours of pain-free sleep for him."

"Okay. I'm a believer. Laughter can be used to eliminate or decrease workplace pain. I can sure use that!"

"Glad to be of help. Now . . . I have an appointment with a water blaster!" George began wriggling his toes into his sneakers but he suddenly flung them off.

"Agagh," he gasped.

"George, what was in your sneakers? A bee?" asked Wonder concerned for his safety.

"No, no. Only my pride has been stung," George said, removing his shaving-cream covered toes from his designer sneakers. "Maggie's going to pay for this," he said running off with a water-blaster poised for squirting.

"See you, George, and thanks," Wisdom shouted after him.

"Yeah, thanks," echoed Wonder.

"Good luck, Wonder," George shouted, glancing back and waving an OK sign with his fingers.

Wisdom and Wonder settled down and continued talking.

"Wonder, sometimes the tests and the teachers in the workplace class-room are very difficult. Our emotions can be so strong that we contemplate death, drugs, alcohol, food, or sleep to remove ourselves from that pain. But, we can reach for humor instead. Those endorphins will instanta-neously release us from the pain until it eventually passes."

"Thanks for the advice and for the introduction to George."

"Sure. When we walk the talk, I'll show you practically how to hallow your humor."

"I look forward to it."

"Now, though, let's have some refreshments." Wonder followed Wisdom back into the house, a slow journey as she stopped and chat-ted with her guests along the way.

## Hallowing the Psychological

> *. . . the most fundamental, most important function of humor is its power to release us from the many inhibitions and restrictions under which we live our daily lives.*
>
> *Harvey Mindess,* Laughter and Liberation

> *Laughter and tears are both responses to frustration and exhaustion . . . I myself prefer to laugh, since there is less cleaning up afterward.*
>
> *Kurt Vonnegut*

> *Humor, then, is a set of survival skills that relieves tension, keeping us fluid and flexible instead of allowing us to become rigid and breakable, in the face of relentless change.*
>
> *C.W. Metcalf*

As they walked toward a different set of French doors, wind chimes tinkled a friendly greeting, filling Wonder with a sense of calm amid all the festivities. When they entered the room, the richness and dimension of the wallpaper leapt out at Wonder. This room was brushed with an Oriental touch and the furniture seemed exotic and intriguing. Swelling pink and white clusters of peonies graced the center of a polished, lacquered table.

He was curious about who else among the many guests knew the significance of those flowers. Naively, he imagined it was a secret only he and Wisdom shared. She sensed his recognition and replied with a quick wink.

Soothing music filled his upper body and he let it calm his mind.

Noticing the company president, Wonder hoped he and Wisdom might tag along in that conversation. He inched his way over toward the president hoping Wisdom would follow. He might finally be noticed by someone big — a sure-proof way to accelerate in his career race. Wisdom didn't pick up on his cue and instead moved closer to the table — very close to the peonies.

Naturally, he followed, but stopped short. He stared at the table. "Oh, geeze!" he exclaimed.

His eyes tried to focus on the hoards of black dots on the table. They looked like piles of ants taking over Wisdom's table cloth. Soon the other guests' attentions also focused on the transformation. Even the president stopped mid-sentence to turn with the crowd. *What on earth would Wisdom do?*

Sing, of course! Wisdom launched her delicate voice into song: "The ants go marching one by one harah, harah; the ants go marching one by one harah, harah. The ants go marching one by one, the little one stopped to suck his thumb and they all go marching on to the sound of the drum boom, boom, boom."

Immediately, the president's voice and that of others continued the chorus as Wisdom and the personnel director removed the peonies, the obvious transport for the uninvited visitors, and table cloth to the outdoors. Conversations resumed.

"Wisdom, that was magical the way you changed a potentially stressful event," Wonder complimented.

"Ah, Wonder, thanks. No magic involved though — only humor."

"And I suppose there's a subtle lesson for me to use humor to ease tension in the workplace? Wonder surmised.

"You got it! You can use humor as a powerful tool to hallow the psychological aspects of yourself or the workplace."

"Are there any actual medical effects of humor on the psychological aspect of our being?"

Wisdom nodded. "Humor is a coping mechanism that helps us mentally deal with the various tests and teachers in the workplace. Again, Wonder, I'm going to reference some medical experts. Cousins also talks about Dr. Annette Goodheart, a Santa Barbara psychologist, who feels that humor helps people to deal with challenges in a more relaxed and creative manner. And Drs. Rod A. Martin and Herbert M. Lefcourt studied the correlation between humor and stress. They found that people who had a greater degree of humor were more capable of coping with severe stresses in life."

"How does that relate specifically to our career classroom?"

"A challenging workplace teacher might say silently, 'Ah ha — you thought you were such a good spiritual student, respond to this one now!' During that moment when that teacher motivates us, we must remain relaxed, keeping our peace of mind and being creative in how we interpret and respond to that challenge. Humor often helps us in this situation. Humor can help us pass a lesson so that it does not have to be repeated."

"Sounds like humor is to keep our minds from overloading on the negative, reactive way of responding and help us remember the answers to our spiritual tests."

"Right on, Wonder!"

Wonder looked around the room. *I've just got to work the room,* his mind raced nervously about being on the fast track. Networking was important. *Why, there was the president again and others from the company and who knows what kinds of contacts her friends had.*

*Someone here may hold the winning ticket for my career advancement,* he fantasized. He caught a glimpse of the president vanishing into the living room for some food; Wonder decided to do the same.

"Wisdom, are you feeling hungry yet?" he queried.

"I suppose I could go for a bite to eat. And something tells me you could too. Let's walk over to the living room, Wonder."

His eyes digested the banquet of colors, foods, and aromas. He selected cheeses, crackers, fruit, and vegetables to adorn his plate.

*All right!* he thought when he saw Wisdom stand near the president; *my fantasies have come true.* He attached himself to her side; he knew that he would maintain a quiet stance, taking in every word from the president. He enjoyed occasionally capturing the president's polite glance while listening to the conversation.

Everyone was commenting on the delicious cherry tomatoes. These were home grown by his teacher, and he mused they might even contain seeds of wisdom! Wonder didn't want to appear greedy so he had selected four tomatoes even though he longed for eight. He would enjoy the full flavor of each very slowly. He felt the smooth tight skin of the first roll on his tongue and roof of his mouth as it pulsated, awaiting the burst. The feat was accomplished as Wonder's teeth reveled in puncturing the skin.

Simultaneously, as Wonder bit into the savory cherry tomato, juice and seeds hurled toward the fine hairs that aligned the president's Adam's Apple. Silence reigned and eyes punctured Wonder. Pain tightened around his head and a sting bivouacked in the roof of his mouth. Heat seized Wonder's brows as he stifled the tears. If only blinking could make him invisible. He had no choice but to surrender to it all. And it all seemed so real.

Wisdom lightly patted Wonder's back as she offered a gold and white angel napkin to the president.

"Sir," she soothed, "quite the experience we dream about in our nightmares." The president smiled and nodded.

"I guess you could say that Wonder has a big heart for he believes in sharing that which he most enjoys."

She offered a humble smile that was met with a large smile.

"Wonder, thanks for sharing," the president said as his hearty laugh was echoed around the room.

Wonder sighed in the outer and in the inner. "Thanks, I owe you big time, Wisdom," he whispered.

"Glad to help. And by the way, you don't owe me. Whenever I give to you, there are no strings attached. Please remember that."

"Gottcha. How could I forget unconditional giving?" Wonder unobtrusively placed the three remaining cherry tomatoes in a napkin in his pocket. He finished the remaining items from his plate, eager to leave the room.

Instead, Wisdom introduced him to her dear friend, Vivian, a vice president of marketing at a large conglomerate.

"Vivian has been very successful throughout the years and is always on the lookout to hire good marketing folks," Wisdom disclosed and winked. "I need to touch base with some friends over there so please excuse me for a few minutes."

Wonder enjoyed a brief and interesting conversation with Vivian and then made a quick stop at the rest room only to find a broccoli floret petal wedged in the upper corner of his front tooth.

"I don't believe it. I am sure making myself unforgettable not only to the president but now to Vivian. Will the challenges never end?" he asked into his reflection in the mirror.

He decided to locate Wisdom and move to a group of people who had not been entertained by his unplanned antics. He found Wisdom tidying up the buffet table. He walked quietly behind her, patting her on the back in the same caring manner she had practiced earlier.

"Oh hi, Wonder," she spoke without looking.

"Hi, there."

"Something tells me that we might want some totally different scenery to complete our conversation this evening."

"You're right on, as usual. What did you have in mind?"

"Well, do you remember seeing the island when you walked in my house?"

"How could I miss it or forget it? The one with the flowers and the waterfall."

"That's the one. There were also two benches on the island."

"The white wrought iron benches."

"Those are the ones," she said. "How'd you like to join me as we each enjoy a bench?"

"Okay. Lead the way," he brimmed with happiness.


HALLOWING THE SPIRITUAL

> *If you wish to glimpse inside a human soul and get to know a man, don't bother analyzing his ways of being silent, of talking, of weeping, or seeing how much he is moved by noble ideas; you'll get better results if you just watch him laugh. If he laughs well, he's a good man. . . .*
>
> *Dostoyevsky,* The Adolescent

> *If you can find humor in anything, you can survive it.*
>
> *Bill Cosby*


He followed her, pausing during interruptions as she exchanged handshakes or friendly kisses with those along her path.

He was impatient to continue their discussion, but he knew she had to be courteous to her guests. Finally, they made it outside. He tried to memorize the stepping stones, the flowers, and the movement of the waterfall. The sound of the crickets tranquilized his thoughts. He would like to recall all of this in the future.

"Wonder, you may take whichever seat you'd like."

"Thanks. I'll sit here," he said landing on the bench closest to the waterfall.

"I figured it might be best to 'debrief' out here about our time in the living room. You certainly have had an interesting experience."

"Experiences are more like it," he corrected.

She tilted her head while raising her brows.

Wonder filled her in on the cruciferous vegetable episode, and they both had another good laugh.

"So, Wonder, what have you learned about humor from your adventures?"

"Hmmm. I suppose I learned that I could have what I think are the most magnificently designed plans to make my career take off and then something I don't even expect can thwart those plans."

"Good. Good. What else?"

"I guess I also learned that when plans for my career don't always go the way I want them to go, I can feel bent out of shape. That pain can be so deep — almost penetrating beyond the physical to some-where else. From a mental standpoint, I guess I just lost it. And then, I felt a peace that originated from deep within — deeper than the pain — if that makes any sense."

"It does. Another good observation, Wonder. And in that particu-lar instance of deep pain, what helped?"

"Well, *you* of course," he chirped gleefully. "Also, I guess it was humor."

"You guess?"

"Okay, okay. I know it was humor."

"So what I'm hearing you say, Wonder, is that you've experienced humor that penetrated the physical and psychological part of yourself to link you to your spiritual part which helped you to feel better."

"Why, yes. And I think you're helping me to say that humor touches our soul and eventually our God nature. It seems to me like humor is similar to meditation for both are avenues we can use to join us with our inner kingdom."

"Absolutely!" she exclaimed, realizing that their teaching/learning project was nearing completion. Although she was pleased to see her student graduating to the next level, the opposites of sadness and exhilaration momentarily pressed her heart.

"Humor tickles the soul. Unlike the physical, the soul does not experience humor via a laugh. Instead, the soul experiences humor as a lightness or swaying from within. There may also be an inner feeling of peace as you've felt. This transcends from the soul into a uniting of the spiritual, absolute grasp of humor as peace and serenity."

Rubbing his chin, Wonder spoke as he gazed into the rustling remnants of the waterfall, "Just out of curiosity, what sorts of humor does the soul enjoy?"

"The soul does not choose a particular type of humor like the intellect does. Rather, it experiences humor as it is interpreted by the intellect."

"So, the soul is just the recipient of humorous feelings?"

"That's right. By the way, I forgot to mention that there is an interesting side effect of humor that is used to hallow the spiritual."

"Just what might that be?"

"Well, consider the axiom, 'What goes around, comes around.' It applies here also. When we give humor to hallow our spirituality, we receive humor in return. Instead of getting angry or sad in the workplace, we can reap the benefit of automatically being able to lighten up and see the humor in the situation."

Wonder nodded his head in concurrence. Wisdom began to rise, and then sat quickly as she recalled another aspect of spiritual humor.

"By the way, Wonder, through the years I have discovered that there is a sense of humor within the universe. Sometimes people or events just happen to get staged in our lives in a practical-joke sort of way. It's fun to look for these, and laugh at them as jokes from the universe," Wisdom said.

Wonder understood. He recalled the waiter in the restaurant where he and Wisdom had gone to discuss the topic of love. *Coincidence?* he asked himself.

"This is all great information, Wisdom, but it seems like the most difficult part to apply. How do I get started?"

"Well, Wonder, why don't you hang around after most of the other guests have left. I've invited a few people to stay. Perhaps we can talk about different ways to do that."

"Sounds great. In the meantime, I'd better go 'network.' Between the broccoli and the tomatoes, I really haven't had much time!"

"Understandable," Wisdom chuckled as they walked back through the house to the backyard.

## WALKING THE TALK

Later on, when the party had dwindled to small groups of conversation, Wonder found himself at the patio table with a few of Wonder's friends and one co-worker, an affable fellow named Smiley who worked in the mailroom.

"So how about sharing some humor aids for business situations?" Wonder asked.

Before Wisdom could answer, Smiley jumped in.

"Comics. Definitely comics. They will lighten any serious situation," he said. "I usually keep one up my sleeve for really difficult meetings with the boss." And to his word, he rolled up his sleeve and to everyone's amazement, out slid a favorite Sunday comic strip.

"This is one that I've secretly shared with my peers. All of you have probably been in the situation when a boss criticized a peer in front of others. Sometimes you don't know what you can do after you've just heard and seen your pal get humiliated. You want to say or do something to help your pal but the boss is still around. In those times, I like to secretly pass this folded up comic to my pal so he can feel relief and regain composure."

"DURING THE BREAK, WE WERE TALKING ABOUT THE TIME PROFESSOR RAINERI CRITICIZED A WITCH DOCTOR IN FRONT OF THE ENTIRE TRIBE."

"Do I have great friends or what?" Wisdom whispered with a smile, laughing as heartily as everyone else. "But," she said, "you can post them in more places — and less cumbersome private ones such as books or desk drawers."

"Oh, Wisdom, honey, get out your collection," said Red, a bubbly looking woman with brassy, rust-colored hair and flamboyant, jangly earrings.

"Yes, yes," a few others echoed.

"Oh, if you insist, I'll be right back," Wisdom said disappearing down the hall.

"Here, quick, put this under the pillow on her seat," Smiley said producing a whoopee cushion. They all giggled.

When Wisdom returned, and after everyone had another good laugh at her expense, she opened an album containing a large collection of jokes and comics.

"I keep my favorites in here, with notes and stuff about laughter and play. I use it at home with the children and also for business. But I also keep a part for cartoons and jokes about the business world."

They all looked through the cartoons.

"So why these particular ones? What do they signify to you?"

"Well, this one is effective if employees want to succeed yet the traditional ways to get there seem to be blocked. There is always another way to get there."

"Boy, you sure taught me that well," Wonder chimed. Others nodded in concurrence.

"And of course, working for a merger and acquisition company, you all have probably figured that I naturally would have one for this industry."

"Show us, Wisdom," giggled her audience in anticipation.

"I regularly share this one with client employees to add a sprig of humor to a potentially tenuous situation as they wonder what the new culture and people will be like in the company they're now merged with."

"I KNOW, I READ THE SAME MEMO.
BUT, SOMEHOW, I DON'T FEEL GOOD
ABOUT THIS MERGER."

"That cartoonist, Heim, is one of my favorites. Oh, please show us more; show us more," baited Red.

"All right, all right. Why, here's one that you, Wonder, might particularly enjoy — it's geared toward the salesperson."

"AT THIS RATE, I'LL HAVE THE ENTIRE CAR
IN ANOTHER FIVE YEARS."

Wonder and Vivian's laughter rang out over the giggles of the other guests.

"Here, Wonder, this comic is my gift to you as a sort of 'humor starter' for your new career."

"Thanks, Wisdom. I promise you that I will look at this if I ever feel discouraged with my sales incentive program."

"I could keep you here all night with Heim's comics so I better make myself stop with just one more."

The guests booed Wisdom's words.

"Come on, we can get together again and have laughs like this. Now pay attention," she said good-naturedly. "Look. Employees can use this comic to feel uplifted if they are in a tiring, stressful situation to work overtime to meet due dates."

"STOP COMPLAINING... YOU KNEW THERE'D BE OVERTIME WHEN YOU TOOK THE JOB."

"But how do I know what situations are coming up? I can't have comics for all contingencies?"

"But you can, Wonder. By collecting jokes each day. Build a humor file. Or make a humor bulletin board in your office. Put your favorite jokes up there. You'll find that often the right joke is there waiting for you when you need it!"

Wonder looked through Wisdom's comics. He found himself laughing often. He began to make scenarios where each comic might be used.

He found one that focused on employees who have concerns but are unable to express them. The open door policy does not exist in their company. Employees are mistreated, but there is no one to listen to their pain. While the situation is serious and many might not consider it a "laughing matter," he found that the comic might release some of the tension and allow the employees to focus on some creative solutions to the challenge.

The group had a great time laughing and rolling their eyes, especially when a comic hit home.

"There must be other ways, besides comics, I mean," Wonder ventured.

"Sure, there's something called exaggerated imagery," Red ventured.

"What's that?"

"It's when you take the time to visualize a situation in completely contrary form of what it actually is. For instance if your boss is overbearing, imagine him being timid and shy."

"How?"

"Through exaggeration," she said. "Wisdom!"

"Yes, ma'am," Wisdom responded.

"Let's role play."

"Sure. Who shall I be?"

"A salesperson, who has to approach a difficult client. I'll be the salesperson, you be the client."

Red stood up and started pressing her clothes in anticipation of the appointment. She knocked on an imaginary door.

Wisdom pretended she was sitting at a desk. As she heard the knock, she bounded to her feet and rushed to the door.

"Hello, hello. Am I glad to see you!" Wisdom said warmly taking Red's hand and leading her into the office. "I feel so privileged that you were able to stop by my office today. Come, sit down. We're just about out of widgets, and I'm also really interested in your new product line — especially those designer-color widgets. I'm all ears!"

Every one at the table doubled over in laughter. Wonder rubbed his chin and scratched his head. They all looked at him.

"Well?" Wisdom asked.

"Okay, so because this sounds silly, the salesperson lightens up and is able to feel more at ease with the client, and is able to focus on a rewarding experience instead of a negative one?"

They all clapped. And Red slapped Wonder on the back.

"You're right, Wisdom, this one's coming right along!"

"Do another one," Smiley encouraged.

This time Red played a manager who usually had poor listening skills and Tom, a friend of Wisdom's from out of town, took the part of an employee who had been called to Red's office. When Tom entered, Red pretended to buzz her secretary.

"Hold my calls, I have important business here. Now, Tom, please sit down. I am eager to hear about all your ideas. Would you like some tea? A cookie perhaps?"

"Or a croissant!" Wonder chimed in and they all laughed while Wisdom blushed. Her friends knew her weaknesses!

"Okay. I really get it now. What else can I do?" Wonder asked. This time Tom answered

"Mental comics. One of my favorite."

Wonder was no longer surprised at the group's creativity and talent. "And what, may I ask, are those?"

"Well, instead of a whole scenario, it's a quick snapshot, like a one-panel comic. When you become accustomed to doing those, you can pretty much turn around any seemingly disastrous situation and at least get a healthy internal chuckle," Tom said.

"I'm sure, you have an example?"

"Of course. A manager is feeling uncomfortable, say he doesn't know how to handle his employee's creativity. He is not sure how to react to her new ideas. So here's the mental comic: Picture a petite, quiet looking employee standing before a large, powerful looking manager sitting behind his desk. The manager's shoulders blades are pressed painfully into the back of his chair. His feet are grounded on the floor; his hands grip his armchair. He looks terribly frightened. He says through gritted teeth and a forced smile, 'I'm ready for your creative idea now.'"

Everyone laughed.

"How about another one. What about regular meetings?" Wisdom asked.

"Yeah. A monthly managers' or sales meetings. You know the kind that are long, boring, and stuffy. Where someone reads historical or statistical material for hours rather than giving employees handouts that they can review when they choose," chimed in Vivian.

"You mean the ones that begin with everyone whispering, 'Let the torture begin'?" Smiley added.

"And when the meetings are finally finished, employees walk away with headaches and with feelings of being drained both mentally and physically. And their butts ache," Wonder groaned.

"Been there, done that," Vivian interrupted.

"Me too, me too," the others resonated.

"Right," Wisdom said. "Although we can't always change the meetings, we can change our attitudes. Let's see . . . How about imagining helium balloons — greeting everyone at the doorway? Each balloon is an appreciation gift! Or how about imagining a theme to an all-day meeting?"

"Yeah, like hats, or a Hawaiian party, or the '50s, or scary costumes, or casual dress," Red offered. "There'd be music — peppy tunes, not elevator music. You know the kind that invigorates the soul!"

Red did an exaggerated imitation of the Twist, and everyone clapped.

"And," Wonder said, raising his voice above the clapping, "when the presenter gets really boring, water pistols will be available to let the speaker know clearly everyone's opinion!"

Everyone turned to Vivian. "Well?" Wisdom asked her friend. "What's your mental comic?"

"Massage therapists," Vivian answered.

"Huh?" Wonder looked perplexed.

"Two massage therapists who work each half of the room, providing shoulder and neck massages to all attendees. And soon the employees are whispering, 'Let the fun begin.'"

"Right on," Smiley said thrusting his hand into a high five.

"Another use of humor is the collection of jokes and riddles," Wisdom said as she delicately squeezed a cherry tomato between her lips. Seeds and juice did not spew forth. *How does she do that?* Wonder thought, blushing, but no one seemed to notice. He refocused on her words.

"These can be used when your boss is cursing you over the phone, when clients are screaming. Use anything to take the edge off the painful words."

"Ohhhh. Riddles. I lovvve riddles," Smiley said, looking devilish. "What did the grape say when the elephant stepped on it?"

Everyone shrugged.

"Nothing—it just let out a little whine."

"Yuck," Wonder replied.

Smiley wasted no time and retorted with another, worse than the first.

"Why did the man name his hog 'Ink'? Because it kept running out of the pen."

Suddenly the room erupted in a chaos of bad riddles and one-liners. People were laughing so hard that tears streamed down their faces.

"Why did the cookie cry? Because its mom had been a wafer so long," someone said.

"What do cows do on Saturday night?"

"I don't know!" someone else said.

"They go to the moovies!"

On and on it went, until Smiley fell right off his chair, and everyone had to help him up. Wonder was amazed. He had not had so much fun since his frat party days, and there everyone was drunk. As far as Wonder could see, there was no alcohol served at all. These people were naturally high! He was impressed. *(For an expanded list of Wisdom's favorite jokes, see the end of this chapter.)*

## BUSINESS HUMOR

After a while, the room sobered up from the laughing spell and Wisdom served coffee and herbal tea.

"I think what businesses need are regular infusions of humor," Wonder commented.

"There's a whole assortment of humor that can be used in business to lighten the workplace and to build a more positive climate," Red told him. "But sometimes people are afraid to try."

"You're saying that in business, we can intentionally plan to inject humor into the workplace? How?"

Everyone started offering ideas, until Wonder's head was swimming with suggestions. He could never accuse Wisdom's friends of lacking creativity.

Some of the ideas included:

> One from management consultant/writer/ speaker, Fred Pryor, who describes "Lite Brigades," committees that develop humorous ideas to lighten the workplace such as casual dress days or ice cream breaks.

> A Giggle Gang to promote humor within the company. Activities might include initiating harmless practical jokes, purchasing humorous birthday cards for employees and managers, collecting and circulating humorous articles,

organizing after-work trips to humorous movies, showing humorous videos or audio tapes during lunches. (Classical Cluck was one suggestion.)

At team meetings, add visual humor by showing up with pig noses, clown noses, or clown glasses.

At team meetings, each attendee chooses an animal. Whenever an attendee is about to speak for the first time at the meeting, he must first make his animal sound. Then the group collectively makes his animal sound and the speaker continues with his conversation.

Institute a Humor Break on a regular basis (once a week, once a day). During this time, consider playing humorous music or jokes on the intercom. (Examples: Classical Cluck, Day-O, canned laughter.)

Incorporate humoraerobics — which according to C.W. Metcalf in *Lighten Up* are "physical and mental exercises that enhance humor skills. With humoraerobics you make silly noises, peculiar gestures, goofy faces, and somehow survive, too." Invent your own humoraerobics exercises or borrow some from Metcalf such as "The American Bat Face," or "Stand, Breathe, and Smile." These can be done at the start of a team meeting or at a specific time each day when your company's Humoraerobics Buzzer rings.

Begin team meetings by sharing a joke either from the leader of the meeting or from participants.

Managers should express their support of humor in the workplace early on. They might ask an interviewee to tell them something funny: a joke or a real life situation.

Add a humor section to your company's library or, better yet, create a Humor Room. Many hospitals have been adding Humor Rooms. For example, Dr. Stehlin, Director of the Stehlin Foundation for Cancer Research of St. Joseph's Hospital in Houston, Texas, has created a "living room" for cancer patients to enjoy family gatherings, play games, and receive visits from celebrities.

Create a humor comic book consisting of comics on topics such as golf, tennis, holidays, babies, working women, raises, and so on. Instead of placing this Humor Binder on a shelf "until needed," put it out front, on the company's coffee table in the waiting area. Clients will be amused, and employees can locate it whenever they need a dose of laughter. It's also helpful for new applicants who typically have a high degree of anxiety before their interviews.

Create Humor Payroll Inserts. On a regular basis (biweekly, monthly, etc.), include a joke or humorous article in employees' paycheck envelopes.

Let your whole body engage in fun. Move around when you hear music. Be creative, move in new ways. Your energy enjoys this freedom.

Keep props at work to help you to release tension and laugh. Blowing soap bubbles is relaxing and fun. Silly putty, play dough, and toy slime are interesting pastimes and release nervous tension.

Create a Joy or Humor Word List just in case you or others start focusing on negative words and need a dose of positive ones. Consider: JOY, MIRTH, HUMOR, LAUGHTER, SILLY, JOKE, GIGGLE, COMICAL, HAPPY, GLAD, MERRY, DELIGHT, FUN, JOVIAL, JOLLY, TICKLE, SMILE, CHUCKLE, and of course HA HA HA!

"Wow," Wonder said when his newfound friends had finished their flood of ideas. "You people really have thought about this."

"It's necessary, Wonder. No job is perfect, and even though most of us have come to accept the difficult part of our positions, we still need support from spiritual guidance and especially humor to smooth the journey," Red said.

"Now, Wonder," Wisdom told him, "you have a bunch of good ideas and sound, medical reasons to add humor into your life."

"Okay," Wonder responded, "let's hear it for Tomato Surprise and Broccoli à la *bouche!*

## MORE JOKES & RIDDLES

Did you see the guy up in a tree wearing a pin-striped suit? You mean the Branch Manager? *Andrew M. Cook*

What is a cow's favorite place to visit? An a-moo-sement park! *Michael Foulger*

Two rival authors met. One had just published a book. Said the other, "I've read your book and thought it was great. Tell me, who wrote it for you?" The author replied, "I'm so glad you enjoyed it. Tell me, who read it to you?" *Rose Sands*

A man goes to a pet shop to buy a parrot. "We have three," says the clerk. "This blue one speaks four languages and costs $1000, and the red parrot knows six languages and costs $2000. The orange one over there costs $3000 but doesn't talk at all."

"Three thousand!" exclaims the man. "How come so much?"

"Well," the clerk goes on, "we don't know what he does, but the other two call him 'boss.'" *One to one*

A self-employed painter had come upon hard times, and there was precious little work to be found. So when a pastor called and asked him to bid on painting the local church, he was almost too eager. He got the job, but realized afterward his bid was so low he wasn't even going to cover his expenses. Desperate, he decided to water down the paint to boost his profit margin. As the job was nearly finished, the sky grew dark and there was a pearl of thunder. Almost instantly, a raging thunderstorm washed the fresh paint completely off the church.

"An act of God," he said to himself, and he became filled with guilt. "I'm sorry, I'm sorry," he said remorsefully. "How can I make this right?"

"Repaint," said a deep voice from above, "and thin no more."

Why do elephant dentists from Africa have it tougher than elephant dentists from Alabama? Because in Alabama, Tusks a loos a!

Where do sheep go to get their hair cut? To the Baa baa shop!

If people live in condos, where do ducks live? In pondos!

How do you fix a broken jack-o-lantern? With a pumpkin patch!

Why did the chicken cross the playground? To get to the other slide!

Why did Moses wander in the desert for 40 years? Because even then, men wouldn't stop and ask for directions! (Quoted on The Larry Nelson Show)

"This horse is well trained," explained the

salesman. "When you want to go, you say 'Praise the Lord.' When you want to stop, say 'Amen'."

The man mounted and with the command "Praise the Lord" the horse raced away. The rider kept saying "whoa" to no effect. Finally he remembered to say Amen."

The horse stopped right on the edge of a steep cliff. Wiping his brow in relief, the rider declared gratefully, "Praise the Lord." *From the bulletin of the Rotary Club of Laconia, New Hampshire*

Why does an Indian wear feathers in his hair? To keep his wig warm.

Here's a tip for when the boss tells a joke: He who laughs, lasts.

What does a baby computer call its father? Data!

Missie: Daddy, are you still growing?
Daddy: No, dear, why do you ask?
Missie: Because the top of your head is coming through your hair!!

Why was the manager of the pretzel factory fired? Because he tried to straighten things out!

What do you call a camel without a hump? Humphrey!

Why did Mr. Jones sleep under the oil tank last night? Because he wanted to get up oily this morning.

Why do employees of a candle factory have it easy? Because they only work on wick ends.

What kind of corsage did Lassie wear to the ball? A collie flower.

## Items for a Humor Library

Humor videos such as *Humor, Risk, and Change* by C.W. Metcalf.

Humor books such as *The Definition of Farts* by Donald Wetzel.

Humor cassettes such as *The Best of Bill Cosby, Laugh Track* by Dr. Anette Goodheart and Dr. Steve Allen, Jr., or *Laughter Heals* by Edwene Gaines and Bert Carson.

Humorous posters on the walls.

## Bibliography

Cousins, Norman. *Head First: The Biology of Hope.* New York: E.P. Dutton, 1989.

Metcalf, C.W.. *Lighten Up.* New York: Addison-Wesley Publishing Co., 1992.

*I get by with a little help from my friends, I get high with a little help from my friends, Going to try with a little help from my friends . . .*

*The Beatles*

*Realize the great truth that each of us is a droplet of divinity, a spiritual being housed in a temple, the body, which enables us to operate in the heavy density of the material world. We have become so imbued with the 'onlooker consciousness' that we too easily assume that God or our guides will speak to us from outside. But the great truth is that the beings of the higher worlds speak to us within our own thinking. All is thought; in thinking we blend with higher beings.*

*Sir George Trevelyan*

*nine*

# TALKING TO YOUR HIGHER-UPS

On Sunday following Wisdom's backyard gathering, Wonder had gone to the public library to browse through some of the many books that Wisdom had been mentioning to him during the course of his studies. On Monday, he was refreshed and ready for work, although still somewhat down about his "new" position. He was glad to have an already scheduled late morning appointment with Wisdom.

He strolled into her office.

"Good morning! Thanks for a great party. You certainly have some interesting friends," Wonder said.

"Well, thank you. They enjoyed meeting you as well. As a matter of fact Vivian was particularly interested in your career plans. She wanted me to give you her phone number and asked if you might call her sometime! There are some major changes going on at her company," Wisdom said with a quiet smile.

Before Wonder could respond, Wisdom continued.

"Well, Wonder, we're coming to the end of these studies, but not, of course, of learning! Remember how we had tutors in school to help with difficult lessons? We also have tutors in the business spiritual world. They are called angels, souls, or spirits," Wisdom said.

"Yeah, right. This is sounding a little weird to me now."

Wisdom was fully prepared for Wonder's response. She had not forgotten his original hesitation at even considering the spiritual aspect of business, and now she knew he would balk at this discussion of heavenly beings.

"Bear with me, Wonder. You've handled a lot so I ask you to continue to have an open mind. This information is very important. Study aids can take you only so far. You must also seek assistance from the appropriate 'higher-ups' if you want to achieve maximum success in the business world," she carefully explained.

"I'm still interested in success so you've got my interest. How can these beings help me? Like angels. What if I decided to believe in angels? What could they do?"

## Angel Talk

> *Angels are the dispenser and administrators of the divine beneficence toward us. They regard our safety, undertake our defense, direct our ways, and exercise a constant solicitude that no evil befall us.*
>
> John Calvin,
> Institutes of the Christian Religion

> *An angel is a form through which a specific essence or energy force can be transmitted for a specific purpose.*
>
> *Don Gilmore,* Angels, Angels, Everywhere

"Before I answer, tell me what you know about angels, Wonder?"

"Well, I've heard of Guardian Angels. I've also seen pictures of paintings of angels."

"Okay, you have a preliminary idea about angels. Let me share more. The word *angel* is derived from the Greek word, *angelos* which means 'messenger.' Angels are the messengers that connect us to the Divine. They bring us Divine help, ideas, and the like by communicating to us in various ways such as ideas, music, writing, a feeling, or a picture."

"And what do these messengers look like?"

"Actually, angels do not exist as a particular image of a person. They exist as God energy that pulsates at a very rapid speed. When the frequency slows down, angels materialize so that we can relate to them through an image."

Wonder looked puzzled. Wisdom could tell this was probably one of his most difficult lessons so far. She gave him time to think and form the questions she knew were racing in his mind.

"How do *I* communicate with an entity that is invisible?" Wonder asked looking very frustrated.

"By speaking or thinking or . . . through your meditation or prayer."

"And just exactly what I am supposed to say to this angel?"

"You can say 'hello,' 'good morning,' or 'good night' for starters. You can share feelings, affirmations, requests for help. You may speak to an angel just as you would to a dear family member, a friend, or a tutor who is there to help you."

"This is interesting," Wonder said, his voice echoing a slight hesitation. "But, I don't know . . . I mean how can I apply all this?"

"Patience. We'll get there, but first I need to share some other ideas with you."

"Okay. You know the ropes. I'm just a beginner here!"


## Soul Sharing

"There's another way you can get help from angels and divine tutors. You can talk directly to the soul of someone else."

"Talk to their soul? How?"

"Carefully. This is a sacred, intimate process. It is also very powerful since the soul is extremely vulnerable. This technique must always be used for good — with the highest intention of the other person in mind."

Wonder read clearly the sincerity and caution in Wisdom's voice. He nodded his head in solemn acknowledgment that he would follow her instructions.

"Sometimes it may be difficult or seem impossible to communicate with another person. Sometimes the outer covering of ego, anger, hurt, or jealousy gets in the way and is not receptive to words or positive thoughts. Soul sharing is a heavy duty method to penetrate that business person for spiritual reasons."

"So how's it done?"

"First, you must get in a relaxed frame of mind. Practice deep breathing and get into a meditative state. Then gently let your thoughts approach the person's soul. Please remember that the souls of some people are like scared animals. Speak calming, soothing thoughts that discuss your purpose for sharing."

"The sharing begins?"

"Yes, light and sacred thoughts are shared. You may also share sacred thoughts relating to the body or the spirit since the soul understands both of these areas."

"Then what happens?"

"Sometimes the human part of the businessperson will be changed in a positive manner. Sometimes it will require multiple communications."

"So I can improve relationships with a challenging business person without that person even knowing it?" Wonder asked.

"Yes! Sometimes business people think that kissing up to someone or being underhanded will influence a challenging person. Those attempts may work initially, but they usually end up backfiring. Approaching things from a spiritual standpoint is usually foolproof, remembering, of course, that you can't be attached to outcomes."

"Oh, yeah. I remember your discussion on preferences quite well. Are there any other ways to communicate spiritually with other people?"

## THE DIVINE COMMUNION

"Sure. You initiate a communion with the Divine part of another businessperson."

"Really? That sounds like something reserved for priests or nuns."

"Wonder, I hope you realize by now that communicating with the Divine is something anyone can do. It's not reserved for anyone special!"

"Yeah, I know. But saying I can communicate with the Divine takes on a different meaning to me."

"I understand. But the indwelling God is one of your tutors. Don't forget that. You can also write a letter to the Higher Self of another businessperson. Meditation is another good way to communicate with another person on the internal level."

"How do I know the other person's indwelling God is 'on line'? That they can understand me?"

"Unlike the soul, the Divine part of a businessperson is not vulnerable because the Divine essence is perfect and whole, embodying all the attributes of God such as power, confidence, wisdom, and love. It doesn't fear communication for it does not understand fear. When thinking or writing to the Divine, you may ask that the human part of the businessperson be receptive to specific qualities of the Divine."

"Shouldn't I ask for the Divine to help the person to be more loving, harmonious, patient, something like that?"

"No. The Divine, like our angels and God, is already always directing each of us in those and many more areas. It cannot possibly provide any more direction or help. However, the human sides of us may construct blocks such as unhappiness, envy, hurt, or guilt that do not allow us to fully see and use that higher direction. You may communicate to the indwelling God, and ask assistance in moving those blocks. Also ask the indwelling God to help them to remember their truths, Divine love, peace, harmony, honesty, and wholeness."

"What sorts of results would I see?"

"There should be an immediate feeling of peace as a burden is lifted. Just knowing that the higher ups are helping should be calming. The results in another person may or may not be immediate. It depends upon how strong their blocks are."

At this Wonder rose and walked around the room. He stopped by the window before turning to Wisdom. But just as he was going to speak, Wisdom's intercom buzzed.

"Oh, Wonder, I am sorry. Usually I don't take phone calls when we're together, but I am expecting an important one. Please excuse me."

As she said this, she gestured to a corner of her office where she had a small library. "Please, feel free to browse while I take care of this, and then we'll get right back to work."

"Sure," Wonder replied, glad that she didn't just reschedule the meeting for another time, because he wanted to explain some of his ominous feelings about his new assignment.

Wonder couldn't help but overhear whom she was talking with, and he was extremely impressed. It was the president of the company. So that's why she wanted to take the call! He was doubly honored that she had not asked him to leave. At that, he tried hard to shut his ears so as not to even inadvertently eavesdrop on her conversation.

He heard the receiver drop in the cradle, and after a moment Wisdom beckoned him back to her desk. He did not say a word.

"I guess you heard who that was?" she asked.

Blushing, Wonder nodded. "Good news?"

"Why, of course," she said. "And now where were we?"

 "You were just about to give me some practical advice on how to use these three special tutors," he said, not daring to inquire anymore about her phone call.

## Walking the Talk

"Let's begin with talking to your angels. There are infinite ways to converse with your angels or use them as your messengers in the business world. In *The Prospering Power of Love*, Catherine Ponder suggests writing to a person's angel:

"'By writing to a person's angel, you establish in your own thinking a harmonious belief about that person; you radiate your harmonious feeling to that person subconsciously; and you also recognize and bring alive in that person's consciousness his own higher, spiritual self.'

"So consider writing a letter directly to the guardian angel of the challenging businessperson."

"So what might a letter sound like?" Wonder asked. "I bet you have a sample!"

"You're right, I do," Wisdom said as she pulled a piece of paper from a folder and handed it to Wonder:

> Dear Angel of John,
> As you've noticed, the working relationship between
> my manager, John, and me has been less than har-
> monious. He's been taking new accounts and as-
> signing them to himself or to his favorite co-work-
> ers. Because of this, I have felt anger and jealousy.

Dear Angel of John, I ask that I might be receptive to the harmony and love that you and *my* angel can teach me. Every morning when I awake, I shall image my angel emerging from my body and release from it a misty, white carpet whose essence is love and harmony. As I wake up, I walk on that carpet so my feet absorb the harmony and the love that my angel has prepared for me.

I also image you, the Angel of John, emerging from John and releasing a similar misty, white carpet whose essence is again love and harmony. John also awakes and walks barefooted on that carpet so that he, too, absorbs the love and harmony. At different times in the day, I will recall that image of the mist still gently touching the soles of my feet. When John and I meet each other, all of our business dealings are filled with that essence of love and harmony. Thank you, dear Angel of John.

Love and Blessings.

"That's a long letter," Wonder said.

"Such notes need not be long," Wisdom added. "Turn the page over."

On the other side, Wonder found a series of short notes.

To the Angel of Carol,
Please go before me at today's meeting. Let Divine Love and Guidance be present with the angels of Bob, Bill, and Jen.

Blessings, Carol

Dear Angels of Guidance,
I ask that you accompany Michelle and her angels on her interviews this Wednesday. I ask that you guide Michelle to her true place of work that will provide her with career satisfaction and financial abundance.

Amen, Karen

To the Angel of Brian,
I ask that you intuitively locate the best applicant for this position in terms of ability, salary, and quality. Let him or her be found quickly.

Blessings, Brian

Dear Angel of Chris,
I ask that you go before me on my marketing call at XXX Insurance Co. Let financial abundance be attracted to me. Let my services, in return, provide my client at XXX Insurance Co. with financial abundance. I bless this situation as my client and I establish a financial bond that is sealed with Divine love.

With love and abundance, Chris

"These are the kinds of letters you write but don't send. They're really like little prayers!" Wonder observed.

"Absolutely. You may also try other approaches. For instance assigning different company positions to your angels. These may be positions held by others who need extra help or positions that don't exist but are needed."

"Such as?"

"Well, if you were responsible for recruiting employees, you might like to assign some angels to be the recruiters for your company."

"So do you actually talk to these new angel recruits? I mean this sounds like a little too much fantasy for me!" Wonder exclaimed.

"It's an exercise, Wonder. It helps you keep your mind focused on the spiritual aspects of being, so that you can achieve your highest good. Remembering to thank all the manifestations of higher beings that help us in our life and our work is not fantasy. It is an important part of the inner work. It may sound silly to arrive at work and bless those divine beings but it has a powerful effect."

Wonder thought about all this for a minute, and while Wisdom noticed that he looked far from convinced, he seemed less embarrassed by the prospect. She decided to continue.

"Remember, too, Wonder, that Angels like us to lighten up. They notice how much we worry about our jobs, our finances, our success, and our interactions with other people."

"So what do they do to help us? No more whoopee cushions, I hope!"

"No, although it wouldn't surprise me to see a bunch of angels running around with whoopee cushions. But you can turn your worries over to the angels in another way. Write your concerns on an index card. Then, place that card in a special place such as a Bible or a spiritual book that means a lot to you. As you're doing so, tell your angels that you are turning your concern over to them. You might make a gesture of release and say the following words to your angels: 'I freely release any worry energy and give up my concern to you. Blessings. Amen.'"

"I like that idea. Sort of reminds of the worry jar my mom had when we were young. We had to put our worries in it before we went to bed. She said they'd be there in the morning when we woke up."

"It's a very similar idea. Let the angels take care of your worries."

Wonder stretched in his chair, and then Wisdom suggested they walk down the hall for some refreshments before continuing. Back in the office, they moved over to her informal conference area, a few chairs around a table piled high with projects and gadgets.

"So is talking to souls similar to talking to angels?"

Oh, yes. In a place of quietness, get still and establish your oneness with God. Free yourself from any negativity, any extra baggage, because communicating with the soul requires clear consciousness."

"What do I do once I'm in a clear, spiritual mood?"

"You start to share your thoughts with the soul of another. For instance:

> "Hi Jonathan. I love you, I bless you, I behold the Divine in you. I come to speak to you tonight in peace so be not afraid. I invite you to come closer and I will share with you the light of the Divine. I project that light to you and it warms you and strengthens you. I hold you in this light during our time together."

"The soul needs this reassurance?" Wonder asked.

"Absolutely! You'll also notice that the more challenging a businessperson is, the more reassurance his or her soul needs. Once you've established the trust, you go on with your message. For example you might say:

> "I guess that you've noticed when the human part of Jonathan and the human part of me interact, there is tension and our business interactions are challenging. Since you, the Soul of Jonathan, touch both the Divine and human realms, I ask you to help when Jonathan and I have future business interactions. I ask you to focus on the Divine love and peace that is the Divine part of Jonathan. I ask that when I send love to Jonathan during our interactions he will not use mean words or his ego to block that love. I ask you to

help Jonathan to understand his Divine confidence and competency so that he no longer feels threatened by my abilities and so that he no longer chooses to set obstacles in my career path. I also ask you to help Jonathan to be aware of Divine prosperity so that he no longer feels the need to interfere with mine.

"In the silence, I ask you to join me and know these truths for Jonathan through the power of the Divine. And so it is. Amen."

Wisdom concluded her example.

"I noticed you avoided dwelling on the shortcomings of the other person and focused on the Divine qualities. I like that, but I imagine it's difficult," Wonder said.

"That it is, Wonder. These soul conversations are not a place to criticize or harass. They are for communicating your most noble wishes and thoughts for your good and the good of others," Wisdom said.

"So what other kinds of situations might call for this 'soul talk,'" Wonder asked.

"Well, let's see. How about when an employee wants to move on to a better working relationship with more compensation and responsibilities?"

"Wait a minute. It sounds like this employee is running away from the problem manager. I thought we're supposed to bloom where we're planted."

"You're right. However, after we bloom, there's nothing wrong with wanting to be *transplanted*. Instead of blooming alone in the rocks or in the shade, we may want to be transplanted near other bloomers, in fertile soil and in the sun."

"Agreed. So how do you explain to this manager's soul that you want another job?"

"Carefully and with love as with all soul conversations. You should bless the manager and thank him or her for all the lessons you have had while working together Say good-bye in a kind and gentle fashion."

"I never thought of saying, 'good bye' to the soul of a challenging teacher once I knew our relationship would be ending. Is this important?"

"It's not mandatory but I suggest it; souls always appreciate your thoughtfulness," Wisdom said.

Wonder thought about one of the executives in their company. They had never really spoken about specific people before, but Wonder felt very bad for Bill and he wanted to discuss it with Wisdom.

"You know Bill?"

"Of course."

"Well, I feel awful about what's happening to him. How could I communicate with him on a soul level?"

"First of all, Wonder, what is so 'bad' about what is happening to Bill?"

"You know. How they cut his position, after twenty-five years. I mean that must be devastating for him."

"Perhaps it is. Have you asked him about it?"

"No," Wonder blushed. "I don't really know him that well, but still..."

"So you don't really know how he feels, right?"

"Right. Where are you going with this?"

"Consider our conversation here today. What's the best way to proceed?"

"Oh, I get it. I'm supposed to talk to him on a scared level."

"And what are the qualities of the indwelling God?"

"No judgments, no anger, no resentment, and all that stuff."

"Right. And?" Wisdom prompted.

"And I will instead acknowledge that Bill is attracting his greater good. And I will share my confidence and trust in his higher self's ability to know and fulfill his truths. Something like that?"

"Yes," Wisdom said proudly, "something like that."

"There's so much to learn."

"There certainly is," Wisdom acknowledged, glancing at her watch. "It is past lunch time — according to my stomach and my watch!"

Wonder was a little disappointed, He had wanted to talk to Wisdom about the foreboding new job he had to do, but she seemed eager to leave.

"I'll be tied up most of this week, with budgets and changeovers. And I'm sure you'll be busy getting adjusted to your new position! Can we wait until next Monday to meet again?"

His disappointment deepened. Monday was a whole week away! He tried to overcome his anxiety.

"Yeah, sure. I guess I have a lot to do as well. Learning to be of service and all."

"And don't forget to practice talking to souls and angels!" Wisdom cheered.

BIBLIOGRAPHY

Ponder, Catherine. *The Prospering Power of Love.* Unity Village, Mo.: Unity Books, 1966.

*Employees get badly bruised, but the attitude is, 'Oh, well, they'll get over it.'*
  *Harry Levinson, the Sigmund Freud of business executives, on his discussion that managers have a lot to learn.*

*There comes a time . . . when we must grab the bull by the tail and face the situation.*
  *W.C. Fields*

*However deep you fall, you are never out of God's reach.*
  *Anonymous*

*ten*

# REVELATIONS

The week went quickly, and Wonder forgot his frustration and anger while digging into his new responsibilities. He tried to be as helpful as possible to his co-worker who seemed congenial and glad to have Wonder's input on creating proposals for presenting to new clients. By Friday afternoon, they were exhausted. They had spent the better part of the day laying out grids and organizing sales tools in the conference room, and when Wonder returned to his cubicle, there was a message from the division manager: his boss's boss!

*How odd,* Wonder thought. He answered the call right away and when he was invited to the division manager's office, he was intrigued and surprised. Wonder wanted to call Wisdom before the meeting, to ask her advice, but he did not want to interrupt her. After the meeting, he could hardly what to talk with Wisdom, and he would have called her at home except that he knew she was away for the weekend. Finally, Monday arrived, and he found himself seated in Wisdom's office, sipping a hot cup of lemon tea and munching on a croissant.

"Guess what?" he grinned.

"I'll guess it's good based on the look on your face!"

"The division manager invited me upstairs on Friday for a little chat! He has been watching me! It seems like my boss expected me to quit when I got passed over for the promotion. And he was really surprised when I stayed and got into the job. This whole episode did not escape the division manager, who said he has been watching me all along . . . *And*, he was impressed that I had been spending time with you. He said it was good for my career to model myself after someone like you!"

The whole time Wonder was rambling, Wisdom sat demurely back in her seat, smiling as if she had just witnessed creation. And in a way she had. Wonder had blossomed before her eyes into a confident and stable young man. He had persevered and was now reaping the reward. She knew he would experience other setbacks, but he was well on his way to putting into practice the many lessons they had studied during the past few months.

"So, Wonder, what was the purpose of the meeting? What did the division manager want?"

"They want to open a sales office in Minnesota, and he asked me to do it. I'd be an official Marketing Representative!"

"And you're excited?" Wisdom asked, slightly surprised. A few months ago, Wonder would have thought they were punishing him by sending him to Minnesota, and he would have quit and started on the low rungs of another company. Now he saw opportunities everywhere, even under mounds of snow and ice.

"Yes siree, I'm excited. Even if it is 40 below up there. I'm going to be a marketing rep!"

He stood up and danced a little jig around the chair and sat down. Wisdom laughed.

"I hope you negotiated for a clothing allowance?"

"Wow, I didn't even think of it," Wonder said sobering up.

Wisdom laughed again.

Wonder explained more of the details and the timing, and then Wisdom spoke.

"Did you ever reach Vivian?"

"Oh, yeah. I almost forgot. We had lunch. It was great. She even offered me a position — that was before I knew about this new deal — anyway, I told her no."

"I'm surprised, Wonder," she said, sounding not surprised at all.

"Remember the reason I came to you in the first place? I told her I needed to stick it out here, to see what might happen. I didn't close the door, though. I told her that she should look at this way: I'd be getting a lot of experience at someone else's expense, and maybe there'd be a position with her company in the future."

Now it was Wisdom's turn to dance.

"You *are* a good salesperson, Wonder. Now what would you like to talk about today?"

"Wow, you're asking me?"

"Sure, Wonder. You have obviously been a good student. So now you can direct some of your own studies."

Wonder thought for a moment and rubbed his chin in his characteristic way as he stared out the window.

"Well, Wisdom," he began, "I have always wondered, were you always so wise? Were you born this way?"

"Of course, like everyone else, I was born wise. The God within us is absolute wisdom. However, I was not always *aware* of that wisdom, and therefore, did not express it. I acquired wisdom through a long process of unsuccessfully *and* successfully dealing with pain."

"So all this stuff — the study aids, the tutors . . . you've learned firsthand?"

"Why, absolutely! How could I ever teach or advise if I had not experienced the workplace challenges and experiences?"

"If it's not too personal, would you share your story?"

"You don't want me to have *any* secrets, do you? Just kidding. I'll be glad to share. I suppose it's appropriate to begin with 'Once upon a time.'"

They both laughed. And then Wisdom continued.

"As you can imagine my soul was educated in the corporate classroom of a merger and acquisition firm. My initial interview was very uncomfortable, and I was ready to walk out based solely on intuition. As that wouldn't have been very professional, I stayed through the interview and in the end accepted the job. That manager, Bullard, gave me the hardest lessons and tests I have ever had. But I never flunked and I never dropped out."

"Bullard? Bbbut . . ." Wonder's surprise bubbled from within and he had trouble finishing his sentence.

Wisdom smiled slowly. Amusement danced in her eyes. She enjoyed Wonder's unabashed amazement.

"All that stuff you mentioned before about your boss and everything? All that has happened right here?"

"Yep," Wisdom answered simply, letting all this sink in.

"Have you had other teachers here?"

"Oh, no. Bullard's been my teacher for years. He often gives me repeat lessons, and I've gone through the pain of studying and trying to master some of the most difficult subjects he's taught."

"Are there any of Bullard's other students still with you?"

"Oh, no. Most don't last three months. They end up switching to other teachers. In fact, there was a standing joke that his classroom had a revolving door since so many students were coming and going from it."

"So what's so good about this guy?"

"When I joined Bullard's classroom, I admired him because he knew so much about this niche in the corporate world. He worked such long hours and without any thought of compensation in mind, I volunteered to help him with some of his work. Bullard did not respond well."

"Why? I thought he would have been pleased," Wonder said.

"He later told me that he was threatened by my offer. He was convinced I was after his job. Consequently, many of my actions and words were misinterpreted to support his belief that I was trying to undermine him to get his position. He used his power to block me and to misrepresent me during conversations with the company president. I never had the opportunity to show them who I really was — a spiritual, loving person with pure intentions."

"What was your reaction to those false accusations?"

"Sadness and confusion. I was just a student in his classroom, and I respected him for his knowledge. He is exceptionally analytical and detail-oriented and very good at organizing.

"In addition to blocking you, did he express fear in other ways?"

"Absolutely. Bullard gifted me with numerous tests, quizzes, and exams."

"Like what?"

"Well, at one point he decided to create a new position in management. This person would assist him with his responsibilities. I had been with the company the longest of those in line for the position, was well liked by my clients, and had developed successful transition plans that were rated 'outstanding' by my clients. But Bullard promoted a new employee, Sly, who had not developed a track record with clients."

"How did Sly do?"

"Sly was one of those people who used a lot of jargon to sound impressive. He'd listen to buzz words and use them in sentences. He'd get other people to do the work Bullard gave him. Sly also had a habit of verbally sexually abusing women — at our office and even at clients' offices during transition planning sessions! He was typically late and he'd leave early to run personal errands. He would pretend to look busy by arranging papers around his desk if he knew Bullard would be stopping by."

"This guy sounds like a combination of all the examples we've talked about over the last few months. He sounds like the mega-lesson of the century!"

"Oh, there's more," Wisdom said. "When Sly interacted with people he managed, the employees sometimes quit, cried, or actually got ill. Somehow I became a sounding board people turned to for advice and comfort.

"Sly's poor management style was actually what motivated me to become a manager and to learn and study positive management techniques. I learned then that the power given to a manager must be used carefully and responsibly. Bullard and Sly taught me in their own way — by misusing the power they had been trusted with!"

"Lessons I'm sure you'll never forget," Wonder said.

"You are right! However, my desire could not materialize because Bullard was mesmerized by Sly. I watched and listened as Bullard attempted to groom Sly by working closely with him and sharing plans and ideas with him. I longed for that to be me."

"So what did you learn from watching what you so dearly wanted being given to someone else?"

"I thought about some wise words from Ken Keyes: 'To be upset over what you don't have . . . is to waste what you do have.' These words became part of my being as I concentrated on the business I did have. I never gave up that management desire; I sheltered it in my heart. I used the waiting time to prepare by reading books, attending classes, interviewing people, and creating binders full of management ideas."

"Have you had any tests from Sly?"

"Yes, but usually they were initiated by my teacher, Bullard. I can recall having to undergo a performance review from Sly. I must say, at that time, it was a humiliating experience. However, Bullard had completed the review and Sly was just there to discuss it with me. I asked why I had received such low ratings and such a minimal salary increase."

"And what did Sly say?"

"He just parroted Bullard, who it seemed had chosen to penalize me for being a quick, productive worker. Designing faster transitions didn't make sense to Bullard, because if I worked faster and more efficiently, the client was billed less, which meant less money for the department; therefore I was penalized by receiving a low pay increase."

"Seems like backward thinking to me," Wonder commented.

"When I called Bullard to discuss the evaluation, I mentioned that it was my goal to be the best merger specialist I could be. In order to do that, I told him, I would need his ideas on how I could improve. Bullard said that he couldn't recall why he assigned the low ratings, but nevertheless, the low ratings and the low compensation remained unchanged."

"What could you possibly learn from receiving an unjust performance review? How could you grow spiritually? Most people would have just quit . . . or gone to the next higher up!"

"In a manner of speaking I did. I went to the highest up! The spirit of the Divine within me."

"Oh yeah," Wonder said, suddenly remembering that he need never feel alone in his corporate climb.

"I learned a lot about self-appreciation too," Wisdom continued. "I knew I might never receive appreciation from Bullard so I looked to myself for recognition and encouragement. I learned to listen to my superior's criticism but to discern what to use and what to discard. And I learned that there is no such thing as loss. Sooner or later it would be my turn to reap rewards."

"Were you the only one who had a problem with Sly?"

"Oh no! Employees were begging me to go to Bullard to disclose the behavior of Sly. They selected me because I had known Bullard the longest. As you can imagine, I was not sure I wanted this task."

"I can relate to your hesitation to offer employee feedback to a superior. That can really backfire. What did you do?"

"I made a list of reasons — pro and con — for confronting him."

To no surprise to Wonder, Wisdom presented him with a piece of paper.

"I still have the list. It often applies to other situations, and it has helped me through a number of similar decisions."

REASONS NOT TO TELL

> Current relationship might worsen.
>
> I could be labeled as a troublemaker, a snitch, or a liar. I could be considered jealous or emotional.
>
> My working conditions might worsen.
>
> I could be fired later for a trivial mistake.
>
> Since Bullard put Sly in that position, how would it look if he had to admit to making a mistake and then having to remove Sly?
>
> Other people who have participated in providing feedback said it has never worked.
>
> Bullard sometimes took the blame for employees, as if there was something he neglected to do with his people. Thus, he might try to protect Sly by assuming responsibility for Sly's behavior.
>
> Since all of us have faults, who am I to cast the first stone?

How effective is one person representing nine others?

The odds are against providing feedback from a popularity standpoint. Sly is Bullard's right hand man so Bullard may feel compelled to defend him.

Perhaps I would not like to function as the guinea pig to see if the open door policy does or does not work in my department.

After feedback is provided, even if I didn't get fired, perhaps nothing would be done. Perhaps Sly would be reprimanded and told not to do certain things again. However, he might still be placed back as our manager.

## REASONS TO TELL

From an integrity, courage, and quality standpoint, perhaps it is better to have tried and failed than never to have tried at all.

Nine other employees are being affected. They have asked me for my help.

It is difficult for Bullard to be aware of things that he does not see. I feel bad that he is being fooled day after day and knowing that I could do something about it.

I feel like a coward, as if I'm looking the other way. I'm pretending that I don't hear or see what's happening.

Many employees are faking respect to Sly for they want to get a good review.

Remember the words, "How many miles must a man walk before he can prove he's a man?" So similarly, how many more people must be affected by Sly before it's over? And how many more lists must we keep documenting his behavior before it's over?

Bullard had at various times asked us to trust him, that even if we had bad experiences with other managers or companies, perhaps it might not happen with him. He might be responsive to this feedback.

Providing feedback prevents mass employee turnover. What if one day Bullard walked in and almost everyone were gone?

Sly is a deterrent to productivity. Employees can't fully concentrate on their work because they have to deal with unethical, inappropriate managerial behavior.

"Those are two very thorough lists to consider. What did you decide?"

"I followed my heart and provided the feedback."

"I'm not surprised. What happened?"

"Even though I tried to completely relax before the meeting, and I even did a meditation as I waited in his office, he entered and abruptly changed the mood. 'Let's get this over with,' he demanded, pointedly glancing at his watch.

"As I shared feedback, he opened his mail, read it, perused a list of new clients. I asked if he felt he could concentrate on the feedback while doing those tasks. He assured me he could and that he was simply 'multitasking.' I continued for several hours, offering information from the nine employees."

"Did he write anything down or ask any questions?"

"Bullard took very few notes, telling me that he had a good memory. His face expressed no emotions. When I was done, I stood, thanked him for the meeting, and fastened my coat, preparing to leave. Bullard immediately began making a phone call. I thought it was interesting that he had so little to say to me during our session yet now he was conversing with someone else. Must be that he was just bottling up his words and now was releasing them."

"And?" Wonder said leaning forward in anticipation.

"There was a long period of waiting after that session. During that time, I released the power of words through a positive, free flowing stream of consciousness. I used many of the very techniques we have discussed over the past few months."

"So, what happened? Did he ever talk to you about the meeting or ask you or others for more information?"

"No."

"So what then? Were you fired? Given more challenging work situations?"

"Well, I wasn't fired! However, I was transferred temporarily to another state, to work onsite with a huge company that was merging with an equally large one. The logistics of mapping out the transition stages and then developing new job descriptions and transferring employees took a significant length of time. I was part of the team sent in to work with personnel. The company president felt it was best for Sly and me not to work together so I was the one who was chosen to leave, temporarily, of course."

"So you're telling me that you had to separate from your family to work out of state while Sly continued on with his regular performance? What lesson or good could have been realized from that test?"

"Being alone in a hotel room gave me the opportunity for a lot of introspection and reading. I learned to understand the lessons and how to pass previously failed tests without having to physically take them again. I came to understand a lot about love, forgiveness, humor, Positive Mental Attitude (PMA), self-dependency, self-appreciation, nonresistance, addictions versus preferences, and healing."

"Did you get to come back?"

"Of course. For some time, I continued to work for Sly because Bullard was still not convinced that the statements from the ten of us were true. Then a local client required onsite services, so I worked out of their offices for a while, but I could commute and still be with my family."

"And then?" Wonder asked.

"A few months later, I received a call from Bullard. Sly agreed to leave the company. Bullard asked me to meet with Sly, during my personal time, to gain an understanding of Sly's outstanding work so that I could then complete it! Which I did — still without a promotion!"

"Sounds like the rescuer role."

"Yes, it does!"

Wonder leaned forward and looked quizzically into Wisdom's eyes. "Why do you stay here?"

"Wonder, I love my job. I love championing the concerns of employees who are thrown into chaos and confusion when two companies merge or when one is taken over by another. I love finding creative solutions to the problems of cooperation and team management. I love showing people how they can overcome obstacles and work together to increase productivity through using the combined resources of both companies. And, of course, I love problem-solving, especially those unexpected events that crop up during the implementation of any transition plan."

Wonder did not doubt her love of her job. She glowed when she spoke of it, and Wonder had heard her on the phone to clients. She possessed a genuine understanding of how to smooth over difficult transitions. He continued to listen.

"My lessons here continue, and I have gladly stayed in this classroom to learn as much as I can. And also to be of service to others, such as you."

"I know. And I really appreciate it," Wonder said solemnly.

"I have released various substitute teachers, like Sly and others, as well as various tests and lessons," Wisdom continued. "However, Bullard is still teaching me, although I suspect not for long. From a higher power, I have requested a new teacher."

Wonder looked inquisitive, but Wisdom did not offer any other explanation.

"But surely, Wisdom, the corporate honchos must know all you do? I mean the President was at your party."

"Oh, he knows. I have had good conversations with him — sometimes in the elevator, in the break lounge. One time I even rode in a taxi with him to a meeting, and we had quite a lengthy conversation."

"Have you ever told him what Bullard does? How he behaves?"

"I doubt it would accomplish anything. Sometimes he only listens to the parts of the problem he wants to. He's not very aggressive about ferreting out all the facts. He seems to take the information that conveniently comes his way and he doesn't bother to inquire further, to ask other managers or employees. I would gain nothing by complaining."

"But you could go somewhere else. Have a better job?"

"Maybe. Maybe not, Wonder. There might be someone at the

new job whose lessons are even more difficult than Bullard's. Besides, look around you. I have a very nice office, a decent salary. I come and go as I please. The insurance benefits are great. I've been here long enough to earn three weeks paid vacation. I love my clients and co-workers. And most importantly, I am living my heart's desire! And all I have to do is put up with Bullard."

"Well, when you put it that way . . ."

"And I plan to stay in the corporate classroom for the education of my soul. As far as Bullard is concerned . . . Well, let's just say I believe his soul and mine have decided to switch roles. His will enjoy being a student and mine will enjoy doing the teaching, though not necessarily with each other."

Wisdom smiled and winked at Wonder. "And besides, *you* may have had an intuitive thought. I so enjoy counseling and teaching employees here and at the companies we work with that I may begin some project of my own. As you can imagine, I believe that spirituality in the workplace is an idea whose time has come!"

"I never would have agreed with you a few months ago. But after all you have taught me, I can't agree more!" said Wonder, offering a serene namaste toward his teacher, who softly returned the gesture.

After a moment of reflection, her eyes glistened and she smiled.

"Enough about me," Wisdom said. "Let's work on some plans for your transfer to Minnesota. I have some contacts here in my Rolodex.®"

BIBLIOGRAPHY

Keyes, Ken. *Pathbook to Higher Consciousness.* New York: Living Love Publications, 1975.

*There will come a time when you believe everything is finished. That will be the beginning.*

Louis L'Amour

*And that's the way it is.*

Walter Cronkite

# Epilogue

Hot tea warmed the roof of Wisdom's mouth. She nibbled at a strawberry cheese croissant as she contemplated how perfect and enjoyable life could be. She admired the surprise bouquet of flowers and card her employees had sent "just because." She felt privileged to have a group of interesting and caring employees and clients.

## Sly

The sound of the phone jarred her from her reverie. She put down her tea and answered.

"Good morning!" she said in her usual cheery voice.

"Wisdom! My favorite voice from the past. How are you doing?"

"Absolutely wonderfully," replied Wisdom, her mind grappling to put a face with the voice. Her stomach momentarily knotted, but before she could say anything, the voice spoke again.

"This is your old buddy, Sly here."

Deciding not to take issue with his assessment of their relationship, Wisdom exchanged, "Sly? Well, what are you up to these days?"

"Well, Wisdom, I have some good news. I got lucky and landed a position at your competitor's across the street. I'm not a manager like before when *you* worked for *me*. I'm in PR now! But you know once they hear me talk for a few months, I'll be a manager," Sly chuckled and snorted.

*PR is a good place for someone with gifts such as yours. Perhaps your skills will be honed and shaped into useful and productive avenues,* Wisdom hoped silently, saying a prayer for his success.

"How interesting, Sly, I wish you well with your new job."

"By the way ,Wisdom, you'll never guess what I'm doing outside of work..." Sly baited.

"Writing a book called *Talking Your Way to the Top?*"

"Huh?"

"Oh, nothing. Tell me, Sly, what *are* you doing outside of work?"

"I'm acting!"

"Go on!" Wisdom laughed.

"Why yes! It's in a play called *Godspell.* Ever hear of it?"

"I believe I have," Wisdom commented, a little tongue in cheek.

"I'll be honest with you, Wisdom. I've always felt like I was a natural actor. I'm also auditioning for an experimental theatre group that specializes in acting out business scenarios."

"Go on!" Wisdom laughed again.

"It's the truth. I have found that during rehearsals I have an easy time memorizing my lines as well as pretending to be someone I'm not in front of others. The director was so impressed that he asked if I'd ever done anything like this before."

"Sounds like you've found your niche." Wisdom smiled.

"Yes, I think so. Ooops. Can you believe the time? No one but me knows that my boss cut out of work early today to go golfing with some friends. She asked me to cover for her and get out some press releases that she needs for tomorrow's meeting. Gotta go. I hope you'll come and watch me act?"

"It would be interesting, maybe I will, Sly!"

After Wisdom hung up the phone, she gazed out the window

and marveled at the way life's circles just keep going around and around.

## Bullard

Wisdom rushed down the hallway. She wasn't usually late or hurried, but she realized a slight psychological block may have been keeping her delayed. She was on her way to join twenty-five company honchos to celebrate Bullard's new position in the company. As Wisdom entered the room she observed that the few handshakes and pats on the back for Bullard seemed not to affect him in the least. It was almost as if he did not even feel them, because they didn't have enough clout.

*Someday, perhaps he will,* Wisdom thought and mouthed a small prayer for his soul.

Adorned in his new costume, Bullard eloquently delivered his lines. In the conclusion he said, "I'm choosing this new position because I've got to follow what's in my heart."

His employees and co-workers had never heard such emotion from Bullard. Wisdom surmised that he knew what they wanted to hear and he had done an excellent job of practicing accordingly. Clapping erupted as Bullard sneaked in an unrehearsed line which resulted in what he hoped, more applause. He was obviously enjoying it. Wisdom knew that Bullard felt he seldom received the right amount of recognition. She watched as he gulped in the applause like a thirsty long-distance runner.

As the applause softened, Wisdom prepared to leave. Bullard had left her mounds of paperwork to complete for several upcoming transitions for some of their largest clients.

Her escape, however, was thwarted by the president who beckoned her. "Wisdom, since you've been the longest employed in Bullard's group, please come up and say a few words of what it was like working for him. Come, come on."

Wisdom sneaked a quick glance at Bullard, whose raised brow and whitened face glared at her. *Gosh, I hope he doesn't faint*, she thought as she made her way to the podium.

"Why, of course, sir," she mustered.

Wisdom took Bullard's hand in hers.

"Ladies and gentlemen, as you know, Bullard and I have worked together for ahem years."

"How many years?" retorted a honcho.

"As I've said," continued Wisdom, "Bullard and I have worked together for ahem years. I cannot begin to tell you all I learned from Bullard. He has probably been the most thorough and committed teacher an employee could ever ask for. I can assure you that Bullard would not stop teaching me until he was sure that I learned whatever I needed to be successful."

"Just remember that he followed the advice *I* gave him on how to teach you," interjected his boss. "*I've* been coaching him along."

Scattered clapping echoed around the room.

"Say more, say more, Wisdom," beckoned a honcho.

"Sure," continued Wisdom as she reached for Bullard's hand that had gotten disconnected when he moved around the stage taking his bows. "On a personal level, I have enjoyed Bullard's intelligence, his skills at transitioning, and the times in which we thought aloud. Why, it was like a Tom Sawyer journey of the mind."

The audience applauded and Bullard's boss added nothing for he hadn't coached Bullard in those areas.

"Bullard," concluded Wisdom, "I have nothing more to say but thanks for being there because I needed you in ways you can't imagine." Wisdom took both of Bullard's hands in hers, bowed slightly to him, and returned to her seat. He beamed and waddled back to his seat drinking in the cheers for which he still thirsted.

Wisdom relaxed into a subtle smile that warmed her body, once again marveling at the path of peoples' lives unfolding.

Bullard didn't know it yet, but in his new capacity within the company he would be working very closely with Wisdom's sister, who ran a large bank responsible for many of the financial arrangements of the acquisition clients that Bullard would be administering.

As she exited the banquet, Wisdom realized that she had never thought of Bullard as a flexible individual. *However*, Wisdom mused, *this trait must be in him somewhere — why even veterans of the company said they had never met a teacher as difficult as Wisdom's sister, Integrity. Another small joke of the universe, no doubt,* Wisdom thought.

Integrity required her students to think, to meet their self-imposed goals and objectives, and to excel in a number of other ways. Remedial work was applied regularly when commitments were not met. Sometimes a student who considered himself or herself "privileged" tried to use connections to persuade Integrity to adjust grades or go easy on a student. To these "privileged," she often bestowed long and arduous detention.

She received some transfer requests; however passing was the only way out of the lessons. In rare instances, when students were granted transfers, they found that although they received new teachers, the lessons started by Integrity transferred with them. *A fundamental law of life*, Wisdom affirmed to herself. In the majority of cases, under Integrity's tutelage, one had no choice but to learn about honesty in business and to seek answers from an ethical platform rather than from peers and connections.

Wisdom was glad to have Integrity as her sister, and both enjoyed the love they shared.

WONDER

"Well, I guess this is good-bye," Wonder said, plopping down in the chair in Wisdom's office that he had come to regard as a kind of haven. Tears welled up in his eyes.

Wisdom comforted. "Have a tissue. Even though this is a business, and I could be accused of sexual harassment, is it okay if we shared a heart-to-heart hug?"

"Gosh yes. You've read my mind, as usual," he joked. "And to think that when we first met, I could barely express emotions and now it feels like I can't control them."

As they hugged, each felt the warmth, sadness, appreciation, hollowness, and fullness in the embrace that lasted. Tears and sniffles were unashamed.

"So this is it," whispered Wonder, swallowing hard.

"Yes, it is," whispered Wisdom also. "May I invite you to know that the 'it' also includes the precious fulfillment you've waited for so long since you are getting your heart's desire. It's finally here. Can you believe it, Wonder?"

"Yes, you know I'm glad about my new career, but I already miss you. I guess it always seemed like I'd have you as my teacher and I could stop by whenever I needed advice or pain relief."

"Weeell, you can still have me as your teacher if you need me; I'm just a phone call away. And with my new job I'll even be more accessible. You really may not need me because you're really pretty advanced, Wonder."

"Thanks. And I do wish you well with your endeavor. I know you'll be successful; you wouldn't have it any other way," he smiled. "By the way, Wisdom, I got you a farewell-appreciation gift," Wonder beamed.

"Oh, what a surprise! Shall I open it now?" she eagerly awaited his reply.

"Yeah — I'd like it if you do."

Wisdom delicately removed the bow and lifted the tape from the paper. Unable to guess what rested in the box, she lifted the lid and gently pulled out a crystal seagull.

"Wonder, it is very beautiful! Thanks, so very much," she noticed as she rotated it, how it reflected the sun into tiny prisms of color and light.

"Um. It's my pleasure. I better go though before I mist up again." He smiled through a new wave of tears and gave Wisdom a quick kiss on her cheek. "Namaskar, Wisdom."

"Namaskar, Wonder."

He waved once from the hall and disappeared into the elevator.


## Wisdom

Wisdom's eyes drifted through the windows of her office and rested on a nest occupying a branch in the huge oak tree that shaded the garden below. Questions dove in her mind.

*Challenges,* she contemplated, *are just part of a daily screen that flashes so that one could draw about them, write about them, dance about them, speak about them — capture them, in some way, and then use the captured challenges for the good of others.*

*It was rather like the way a model paraded down a runway, got photographed, and then the photograph was used in an ad or on TV,* she mused. *Maybe that's the way challenges are too. Maybe each screen is refreshed the next day and another scene is acted out, captured, and used.*

Wisdom's thoughts were momentarily interrupted by the mother bird, who flew from her nest, presumably in search of food for her nestlings who would soon be off on their own. Wisdom brought her attention back to the office. She looked around her own nest, stopping to remember conversations and discussions that had taken place in her office. She recalled moments with various students, and found that her most fond memories centered on one of her star pupils, Wonder. She knew they would always remain friends.

While she felt sad to be leaving a classroom that had taught her a variety of valuable but difficult lessons, she was, at the same time, thrilled to be embarking on a new heart's desire. Well, it wasn't exactly new, more like a modification and enhancement of the work she already loved.

Wisdom silently thanked her angels and the higher powers — the Divine forces that supported and nurtured her. She called upon them to continue their lessons and encouragement, and she promised to seek the soul's purest essence at every opportunity.

Although Wisdom had often worked with employee transition teams, the bulk of her work all these years had been in the hard-core environment of the high-powered merger and acquisition department, mapping out strategic plans and meeting hectic schedules of implementation. She now longed to use her skills to meld the spiritual with the business. Wisdom had learned over the years just how important spiritual tools are to the business world, and it would now be her pleasure to show others how to use them.

Wisdom had carefully planned her departure so as not to make any enemies. As a matter of fact, clients she had established over the years were eager to hear about her new venture and many had already invited her to speak to their employees. Even the company president had set aside a meeting time so that she could discuss her new endeavor before leaving the firm. She smiled when she recalled receiving the president's call to schedule this meeting . . . *Inquisitive minds want to know,* she guessed. It didn't matter whether or not he understood or concurred, she was pleased he had expressed interest.

Even though the employees' planned farewell activities had concluded, an ending just wouldn't form for Wisdom. Thoughts of employees — both her own and those she assisted during transitions still lingered. Her thoughts soon shifted to Kierkegard's words that kindled in her mind, "To love human beings is still the only thing worth living for — without love, you really do not live." And she *had* lived with gusto at the merger and acquisition firm for she had enjoyed both giving and receiving love with employees. She whispered a namaste to all employees she had been 'in relationship' with during the ahem years. Before leaving, she whispered some blessings to her office that had nested many of her clients and employees. As she reached to place Wonder's crystal gift in its box, she discovered a scribbled note in which he had quoted from *Jonathan Livingston Seagull*. She recognized the words as being spoken from the Flock that had come to take Jonathan higher: "'One school is finished, and the time has come for another to begin.' [U]nderstanding lighted that moment for Jonathan Seagull. They were right. He *could* fly higher, and it was time to go home. He gave one last look across the sky, across that magnificent silver land where he had learned so much. 'I'm ready,' he said at last. And Jonathan Livingston Seagull rose with two star-bright gulls to disappear into a perfect dark sky." *It figures I'd find that note now,* Wisdom smiled, *not quite a joke from the universe, but close.*

As she drove away, she mentally compiled a list of others who she felt would welcome the seminars and consulting services she was now available to offer without anyone's interference — weeell, except from that unexpected teacher who would probably happen into her life as soon as she was ready for her *new* advanced spiritual lessons.

BIBLIOGRAPHY

Bach, Richard. *Jonathan Livingston Seagull.* New York: Avon Books, 1970.

# BIBLIOGRAPHY

Bach, Richard. *Illusions: The Adventures of a Reluctant Messiah.* New York: Dell Publishing Group, 1977.

Bach, Richard. *Jonathan Livingston Seagull.* New York: Avon Books, 1970.

Blanchard, Kenneth. *One Minute for Myself.* New York: Avon Books, 1985.

Blanchard, Kenneth & Spencer Johnson. *The One Minute Manager.* New York: Berkley Publishing Group, 1983.

Boland, Jack. *Master Mind Goal Achiever's Journal.* Warren, Mich.: Master Mind Publishing Co., 1989.

Borysenko, Joan. *Minding the Body, Mending the Mind.* Reading, Mass.: Addison-Wesley Publishing Co., 1987.

Buscaglia, Leo. *Love.* New York: Ballantine Books, 1972.

Butterworth, Eric. *In the Flow of Life.* Unity Village, Mo.: Unity School of Christianity, 1983.

Cohen, Alan. *The Dragon Doesn't Live Here Anymore.* New York: Balantine, 1981.

A Course in Miracles. Tiburon, Calif.: Foundation for Inner Peace, 1985.

Cousins, Norman. *Anatomy of an Illness.* New York: W. W. Norton & Company, 1979.

Cousins, Norman. *Head First: The Biology of Hope.* New York: E. P. Dutton, 1989.

Ellsworth, Barry. *Living in Love.* Salt Lake City: Breakthrough Publishing, 1988.

Emerson, Ralph Waldo. "Compensation." In *The Harvard Classics.* Vol. 5. Edited by Charles W. Eliot. New York: P.F. Collier & Son, 1909.

Emerson, Ralph Waldo. "Essays on English Traits." In *The Harvard Classics.* Vol. 5. Edited by Charles W. Eliot. New York: P.F. Collier & Son, 1909.

Fillmore, Charles. *Christian Healing.* Unity Village, Mo.: Unity Books, 1986.

Fillmore, Charles. *Metaphysical Bible Dictionary.* Unity Village, Mo.: Unity Books, 1988.

Fillmore, Charles. *The Revealing Word.* Unity Village, Mo.: Unity Books, 1988.

Fillmore, Charles. *The Twelve Powers of Man.* Unity Village, Mo.: Unity Books, 1994.

Fisher, Mark. *Instant Millionaire.* San Rafael, Calif.: New World Library, 1990.

Fox, Emmet. *Power Through Constructive Thinking.* New York: Harper & Row, 1940.

Fromm, Erich. *The Art of Loving.* New York: Harper & Row, 1956.

Gawain, Shakti. *Creative Visualization.* New York: Bantam Books, 1978.

Gibran, Kahlil. *The Prophet.* New York: Alfred A. Knopf, 1979.

Goldsmith, Joel. *The Art of Meditation.* San Francisco: Harper & Row, 1956.

Hay, Louise. *You Can Heal Your Life.* Santa Monica, Calif.: Hay House, 1984.

Hill, Napoleon. *Think and Grow Rich.* North Hollywood, Calif.: Wilshire Book Co., 1966.

Hurst, Kenneth Thurston. *Live Life First Class.* York Beach, Maine: A Mountainvue Publication, 1985.

Jafolla, Richard. *Soul Surgery.* Marina del Rey, Calif.: DeVorss, 1982.

Jampolsky, Gerald. *Love is Letting Go of Fear.* Berkeley, Calif.: Celestial Arts, 1979.

Jampolsky, Lee. *Healing the Addictive Mind.* Berkeley, Calif.: Celestial Arts, 1991.

Jeffers, Susan. *Feel the Fear and Do It Anyway.* New York: Ballantine Books, 1988.

John of the Cross, St. *Dark Night of the Soul.* New York: Doubleday, 1990.

Keyes, Ken. *Pathbook to Higher Consciousness.* New York: Living Love Publications, 1975.

Lunde, Norman. *You Unlimited.* Marina del Rey, Calif.: DeVorss, 1977.

Maltz, Maxwell. *Psycho-cybernetics.* North Hollywood, Calif.: Wilshire Book Co., 1960.

Mandino, Og. *The Greatest Salesman in the World.* New York: Bantam Books, 1988.

Metcalf, C.W. & Roma Felible. *Lighten Up.* New York: Addison-Wesley Publishing Co., 1992.

Mindess, Harvey. *Laughter and Liberation.* Los Angeles: Nash, 1971.

Moody, Raymond A. *Laugh After Laugh.* New York: Headwaters Press, 1978.

Ponder, Catherine. *Healing Secrets of the Ages.* Marina del Rey, Calif.: DeVorss, 1967.

Ponder, Catherine. *Open Your Mind to Prosperity.* Marina del Rey, Calif.: DeVorss, 1983.

Ponder, Catherine. *The Prospering Power of Love.* Unity Village, Mo.: Unity Books, 1966.

Pounders, Margaret. *Laws of Love.* Unity Village, Mo.: Unity Books, 1979.

Price, John. *Practical Spirituality.* Austin: Quartus Books, 1985.

Schwartz, David. *The Magic of Thinking Big.* New York: Simon & Schuster, 1965.

Sinetar, Marsha. *Ordinary People as Monks and Mystics.* New York: Paulist Press, 1986.

Silva, Jose and Ed Bernd Jr. *Sales Power: The Silva Mind Method for Sales Professionals.* New York: Putnam Publishing Group, 1992.

Taylor, Terry Lynn. *Guardians of Hope.* Tiburon, Calif.: H.J. Kramer, 1992.

Taylor, Terry Lynn. *Messengers of Light.* Tiburon, Calif.: H.J. Kramer, 1990

Ziglar, Zig. *Top Performance.* New York: Berkley Books, 1982.

# ABOUT THE AUTHOR

Ellen Raineri has been actively writing and fascinated by quotations since she was a child. She received her first writing award from the Pennsylvania Governor's School for the Arts Scholarship in Creative Writing at Bucknell University in 1977. Since then, she has won various monetary awards for short stories and poetry.

Raineri earned her Bachelor's degrees in English, Education, and Computer Science from Wilkes University and an MBA in Management Information Systems from Marywood College, where she received the sole medal for experience in business. For the past eighteen years, Raineri has used her personal time to study the keys to success and self-help, and for the past fifteen years she has studied spirituality.

She has worked as a business unit manager to market and manage computer consulting services, as a computer programmer, and as an English and math teacher. She regularly teaches classes at Unity centers. Currently, she is the owner and president of Braino, Inc., a business consulting firm. Raineri is available for speaking engagements and offers consulting services including integrating spirituality into business. She can be contacted through Braino, Inc., 227 Seminole Avenue, Wilkes-Barre, PA 18702; 717-825-5601

# ORDER FORM

☎    TELEPHONE ORDERS    717 825 5601

*Please have your AMEX, Discover, VISA, or MasterCard ready*

▨    FAX ORDERS      717 825 6444

✉    MAIL ORDERS      Braino, Inc.

                          227 Seminole Ave, Wilkes-Barre, PA 18702

NAME

COMPANY

ADDRESS

CITY                                STATE       ZIP

TELEPHONE

PRICE    $ 14.95 EACH           QUANTITY OF BOOKS

SALES TAX    PLEASE ADD 6% FOR BOOKS SHIPPED TO PA ADDRESSES.

SHIPPING    $ 3.00 FOR FIRST BOOK,

               $ 2.50 FOR EACH ADDITIONAL BOOK.

PAYMENT    ☐ CHECK      ☐ CREDIT CARD

               ☐ DISCOVER   ☐ MASTERCARD   ☐ VISA   ☐ AMEX

CARD NUMBER

NAME ON CARD                            EXP. DATE